Agriculture Issues and Policies

HIRED FARMWORKERS:
PROFILE AND LABOR ISSUES

AGRICULTURE ISSUES AND POLICIES

Agriculture Issues & Policies, Volume I
Alexander Berk (Editor)
2001. ISBN 1-56072-947-3

Hired Farmworkers: Profile and Labor Issues
Rea S. Berube (Editor)
2009. ISBN 978-1-60741-232-8

Agriculture Issues and Policies

HIRED FARMWORKERS: PROFILE AND LABOR ISSUES

REA S. BERUBE
EDITOR

Nova Science Publishers, Inc.
New York

Copyright © 2009 by Nova Science Publishers, Inc.

All rights reserved. No part of this book may be reproduced, stored in a retrieval system or transmitted in any form or by any means: electronic, electrostatic, magnetic, tape, mechanical photocopying, recording or otherwise without the written permission of the Publisher.

For permission to use material from this book please contact us:
Telephone 631-231-7269; Fax 631-231-8175
Web Site: http://www.novapublishers.com

NOTICE TO THE READER
The Publisher has taken reasonable care in the preparation of this book, but makes no expressed or implied warranty of any kind and assumes no responsibility for any errors or omissions. No liability is assumed for incidental or consequential damages in connection with or arising out of information contained in this book. The Publisher shall not be liable for any special, consequential, or exemplary damages resulting, in whole or in part, from the readers' use of, or reliance upon, this material.

Independent verification should be sought for any data, advice or recommendations contained in this book. In addition, no responsibility is assumed by the publisher for any injury and/or damage to persons or property arising from any methods, products, instructions, ideas or otherwise contained in this publication.

This publication is designed to provide accurate and authoritative information with regard to the subject matter covered herein. It is sold with the clear understanding that the Publisher is not engaged in rendering legal or any other professional services. If legal or any other expert assistance is required, the services of a competent person should be sought. FROM A DECLARATION OF PARTICIPANTS JOINTLY ADOPTED BY A COMMITTEE OF THE AMERICAN BAR ASSOCIATION AND A COMMITTEE OF PUBLISHERS.

LIBRARY OF CONGRESS CATALOGING-IN-PUBLICATION DATA
Available upon request
ISBN: 978-1-60741-232-8

Published by Nova Science Publishers, Inc. ✤ *New York*

CONTENTS

Preface		**vii**
Chapter 1	Profile of Hired Farmworkers, A 2008 Update *William Kandel*	**1**
Chapter 2	Temporary Farm Labor: The H-2A Program and the U.S. Department of Labor's Proposed Changes in the Adverse Effect Wage Rate (AEWR) *Gerald Mayer*	**69**
Chapter 3	Farm Labor: The Adverse Effect Wage Rate (AEWR) *William G. Whittaker*	**117**
Chapter 4	Farm Labor Shortages and Immigration Policy *Linda Levine*	**135**
Index		**159**

PREFACE

This book looks at hired farmworkers who make up a third of the total agricultural labor force and are critical to U.S. agricultural production, particularly in labor-intensive sectors such as fruits and vegetables. The hired farmworker labor market is unique because it includes a large population of relatively disadvantaged and often unauthorized workers, a portion of whom migrate to, and within, the United States. Recent economic and demographic trends are discussed in this book, such as changing agricultural production methods that permit year-round employment, expanding immigrant populations in nonmetropolitan counties, and growing concerns over U.S. immigration policies. This 2008 profile serves as an update to the 2000 Economic Research Service analysis using current data with expanded sections on legal status, poverty, housing and use of social services. Consequently, as examined in this book, hired farmworkers remain among the most economically disadvantaged working groups in the U.S., despite their critical importance to many agricultural sectors.

Chapter 1 - Hired farmworkers make up a third of the total agricultural labor force and are critical to U.S. agricultural production, particularly in labor-intensive sectors such as fruits and vegetables. The hired farmworker labor market is unique because it includes a large population of relatively disadvantaged and often unauthorized workers, a portion of whom migrate to, and within, the United States. Recent economic and demographic trends, such as changing agricultural production methods that permit year-round employment, expanding immigrant populations in nonmetropolitan counties, and growing concerns over U.S. immigration policies, have elicited increased interest in hired farm- workers. This 2008 profile serves as an update to the 2000 Economic Research Service analysis of the 1998 Current Population Survey using current data with expanded sections on legal status, poverty, housing, and use of social services.

Chapter 2 - The H-2A temporary agricultural worker program allows American agricultural employers to hire foreign workers to perform full-time temporary or seasonal work on farms in the United States. H-2A workers must be paid *at least* the highest of the adverse effect wage rate (AEWR), the prevailing wage, or the applicable federal or state minimum wage. The prevailing wage is based on state surveys funded by the U.S. Department of Labor (DOL). The AEWR is based on wage data from the Farm Labor Survey (FLS), which is conducted by the U.S. Department of Agriculture.

On February 13, 2008, the U.S. Department of Labor (DOL) published proposed regulations that would change the way the AEWR is determined. Final action on the proposed rule is expected in November 2008. Under the rule, the AEWR would be calculated from the Occupational Employment Statistics (OES) survey, which is conducted by the Bureau of Labor Statistics of the U.S. Department of Labor and state workforce agencies. Wages from the OES survey are available at four levels of skill and experience. The four wage levels are called Level I, Level II, Level III, and Level IV. Under the proposed rule, the AEWR could not be less than $7.25 an hour. The FLS and OES surveys cover different farm-related employers and provide different levels of detail by occupation and geographic area. An issue for Congress is the impact of the proposed change on the wages and employment of unauthorized farmworkers, H-2A workers, and U.S. workers.

Generally speaking, under the proposed rule, in most areas both the minimum AEWR of $7.25 and the OES Level I wage (for entry level workers) would be lower than the current AEWR. In some areas, however, the Level I wage would be higher than the current AEWR. On the other hand, in most areas, the OES Level IV wage (for workers with management or supervisory duties), especially for livestock workers and farm equipment operators, would be higher than the current AEWR. Compared to the current AEWR, the proposed AEWR is more likely to be lower for crop workers than for livestock workers or farm equipment operators.

In some areas, the prevailing wage could become the highest of the AEWR, prevailing wage, or minimum wage. In some areas in some states, the state minimum wage could become the highest of the three wage rates.

In areas where the proposed rule would lower the wages that employers must offer H-2A workers, the rule should create an incentive for employers to hire more H-2A, as opposed to unauthorized, workers. In areas where the rule would increase the wages that employers must offer H-2A workers, the rule would probably not create an incentive to hire more H-2A workers. On the other hand, in areas where the rule would increase the wages of H-2A workers, it should create an incentive for employers to hire more U.S. workers. However, in areas where the rule would lower the wages that employers must offer H-2A workers, it could lower the wages employers offer U.S. workers. This report will be updated as issues warrant.

Chapter 3 - American agricultural employers have long utilized foreign workers on a temporary basis, regarding them as an important labor resource. At the same time, the relatively low wages and acceptance of often difficult working conditions by such workers have caused them to be viewed as an economic threat to domestic American workers.

To mitigate any "adverse effect" for the domestic workforce, a system of wage floors has been developed that applies, variously, both to alien and citizen workers — the *adverse effect wage rate* (AEWR). Under this system, a *guest worker* must be paid either the AEWR, the state or federal minimum wage, or the locally prevailing wage for his or her occupation, whichever is higher.

An H-2A worker is identified under 8 U.S.C. at 101(a)(15)(H)(ii)(a) of the Immigration and Nationality Act as a nonimmigrant alien seeking temporary employment in the United States. Wages paid to H-2A and related workers are but one aspect of broader immigration questions. In this report, however, the issue is limited to domestic economic concerns. Use of guest workers has evolved from a relatively simple exchange of labor along the frontier between Mexico and the United States, responding to the requirements of local employers, into a far more complicated structure that has expanded nationwide and involves many thousands of workers.

During World War I, Mexican workers were brought into the country to replace draftees. Later, during the Great Depression, those remaining in the States were subject to sporadic repatriation proceedings. During World War II, there was again perceived to be a need for guest workers; and, with the cessation of hostilities, there was also an effort to reduce the flow of aliens to the United States. Since the mid- 1 960s, several new programs involving guest workers have been instituted. In addition, numerous undocumented workers have entered (or re-entered) the country. Collectively, these guest workers, some have suggested, have come to compete with domestic (U.S.) workers — even where those domestic workers could be available for employment were conditions more favorable. Thus, the AEWR has been designed, in part, to deal with a putative surplus of alien workers but also to address any adverse impact upon domestic American workers.

This report is written from the perspective of labor policy, not of immigration policy. For discussion of immigration issues, see the Current Legislative Issues on the Congressional Research Service website [http://www.crs.gov].

Chapter 4 - The connection between farm labor and immigration policies is a longstanding one, particularly with regard to U.S. employers' use of workers from Mexico. The Congress is revisiting the issue as it debates guest worker programs, increased border enforcement, and employer sanctions to curb the flow of unauthorized workers. Two decades ago, the Congress passed the Immigration Reform and Control Act (IRCA, P.L. 99-603) to reduce illegal entry into the United States by imposing sanctions on employers who knowingly hire persons who lack permission to work in the country. In addition to a general legalization program, IRCA included legalization programs specific to the agricultural industry that were intended to compensate for the act's expected impact on the farm labor supply and encourage development of a legal crop workforce. These provisions of the act have not operated in the offsetting manner that was intended: substantial numbers of unauthorized aliens have continued to join legal farm workers in performing seasonal agricultural services (SAS).

A little more than one-half of the SAS workforce is not authorized to hold U.S. jobs. Crop growers contend that their sizable presence implies a shortage of native-born farm workers. Grower advocates argue that farmers would rather not employ unauthorized workers because doing so puts them at risk of incurring penalties. Farm worker advocates counter that crop growers prefer unauthorized workers because they are in a weak bargaining position. If the supply of unauthorized workers were curtailed, it is claimed, farmers could adjust to a smaller workforce by introducing labor-efficient technologies and management practices, and by raising wages, which, in turn, would entice more U.S. workers to accept farm jobs. Growers respond that further mechanization would be difficult for some crops, and that much higher wages would make the U.S. industry uncompetitive in world markets without expanding the legal farm workforce. These remain untested arguments because perishable crop growers have rarely, if ever, operated without unauthorized foreign-born workers.

Trends in the agricultural labor market generally do not suggest the existence of a nationwide shortage of domestically available farm workers, in part because the government's databases cover authorized and unauthorized workers. While nonfarm employment generally has increased thus far in the current decade, farm jobs generally have decreased. The length of time hired farm workers are employed has changed little or fallen over the years as well. Their unemployment rate has varied slightly and remains well above the U.S. average. Underemployment among farm workers also remains substantial. In addition, the earnings of farm workers relative to other private sector employees has changed little over time.

This assessment does not preclude the possibility of labor shortages in particular geographic areas at particular times of the year. Some statistical evidence suggests that California growers experienced a tighter labor market in July 2007 compared to peak harvest season a year earlier. It nonetheless appears that the offer of larger wage increases than those of employers in other industries contributed to there being sufficient (authorized and unauthorized) workers available to enable California growers to increase employment on their farms in the year ended July 2007.

In: Hired Farmworkers: Profile and Labor Issues ISBN: 978-1-60741-232-8
Editor: Rea S. Berube, pp. 1-68 © 2009 Nova Science Publishers, Inc.

Chapter 1

PROFILE OF HIRED FARMWORKERS, A 2008 UPDATE[*]

William Kandel

ABSTRACT

Hired farmworkers make up a third of the total agricultural labor force and are critical to U.S. agricultural production, particularly in labor-intensive sectors such as fruits and vegetables. The hired farmworker labor market is unique because it includes a large population of relatively disadvantaged and often unauthorized workers, a portion of whom migrate to, and within, the United States. Recent economic and demographic trends, such as changing agricultural production methods that permit year-round employment, expanding immigrant populations in nonmetropolitan counties, and growing concerns over U.S. immigration policies, have elicited increased interest in hired farm- workers. This 2008 profile serves as an update to the 2000 Economic Research Service analysis of the 1998 Current Population Survey using current data with expanded sections on legal status, poverty, housing, and use of social services.

Keywords: Hired farmworkers, farm labor, agriculture, migrant, immigrant, farm structure, demography, legal status, employment, poverty, housing, social services, health.

---

[*] Excerpted from Economic Research Report Number 60, dated July 2008.

ACKNOWLEDGMENTS

This report benefited substantially from comments by Philip L. Martin, University of California, Davis; Cornelia Flora, Iowa State University; Bruce Goldstein, Farmworker Justice, James Hrubovcak, the U.S. Department of Agriculture, Office of the Chief Economist; and from the following at the U.S. Department of Agriculture, Economic Research Service: Mary Ahearn, Eldon Ball, Mary Bohman, Robert Gibbs, Robert Hoppe, Carol Jones, Barry Krissoff, Jack Runyan (retired), Patrick Sullivan, and Steven Zahniser. The author also would like to thank Daniel Carroll from the U.S. Department of Labor for access to the most recent and restricted National Agricultural Workers Survey (NAWS) data and Mark Aitken from the U.S. Department of Agriculture, National Agricultural Statistics Service (NASS), for technical assistance and special tabulations of NASS data. Finally, I gratefully acknowledge Angela Anderson for editorial assistance, and Susan DeGeorge for graphics, layout, and cover design.

SUMMARY

Current estimates indicate that more than 1 million hired farmworkers are employed in U.S. agriculture. Economic and demographic trends have elicited an increased interest in hired farmworkers, including the impact they have on U.S. agricultural production. While productivity gains have gradually reduced the total agricultural labor force, hired farmworkers continue to play an important role in this industry.

What Is the Issue?

Hired farmworkers make up a third of the total agricultural labor force and are critical to U.S. agricultural production, particularly for labor-intensive sectors such as fruits and vegetables. The hired-farmworker labor market is unique because it includes a relatively disadvantaged and sometimes mobile workforce, a large proportion of whom lack authorization to work in the United States. Although agriculture employs less than 2 percent of the U.S. labor force, recent economic and demographic trends such as agricultural production methods that permit year-round employment, expanding immigrant populations in nonmetropolitan counties, and growing concerns over U.S. immigration policies have increased interest in hired farmworkers.

What Did the Study Find?

- In 2006, an average 1.01 million hired farmworkers made up a third of the estimated 3 million people employed in agriculture. The other 2.05 million included self-employed farmers and their unpaid family members.
- Productivity gains have gradually reduced the total agricultural labor force and the number of hired farmworkers within it.
- Expanding nonfarm economic opportunities for farmers and their family members have increased farmers' reliance on hired farm labor.
- Despite new patterns of Hispanic population settlement in rural areas, the geographic distribution of farmworkers has not changed significantly in the past decade. California, Florida, Texas, Washington, Oregon, and North Carolina account for half of all hired and contracted farmworkers.
- Hired farmworkers are disadvantaged in the labor market relative to most other U.S. wage and salary workers. On average, hired farmworkers are younger, less educated, more likely to be foreign-born, less likely to speak English, and less likely to be U.S. citizens or to have a legally authorized work permit.
- According to the National Agricultural Workers Survey (NAWS), which offers the most precise data available on farmworker legal status, half of all hired crop farmworkers lack legal authorization to work in the United States.
- Farmworker unemployment rates are double those of all wage and salary workers, but vary considerably by individual characteristics. Those working in field crops have twice the unemployment rate of livestock workers.
- Hired farmworkers earn less than other workers. Median weekly earnings of full-time farmworkers are 59 percent of those for all wage and salary workers. Poverty among farmworkers is more than double that of all wage and salary employees.
- Hired farmworkers who migrate between work locations are disadvantaged in the labor market and earn less than settled farmworkers. Disadvantages include poorer health and challenges to migrant children attending school.

- Housing conditions of farmworkers have historically been substandard because of crowding, poor sanitation, poor housing quality, proximity to pesticides, and lax inspection and enforcement of housing regulations.
- Agricultural work is among the most hazardous occupations in the United States, and farmworker health remains a considerable occupational concern. Farmworkers face exposure to pesticides, risk of heat exhaustion and heat stroke, inadequate sanitary facilities, and obstacles in obtaining health care due to high costs and language barriers.
- Hired farmworkers use select social services, such as Food Stamps, Women, Infants, and Children (WIC) Nutrition Program, Medicaid, and free school lunches, at higher rates than other wage and salary employees. Within the noncitizen crop farmworker population, authorized workers use those services at higher rates than unauthorized workers. Citizen farmworkers, whose poverty rates are a third those of noncitizen farmworkers, use such programs less than authorized noncitizen workers.

How Was the Study Conducted?

Principal data sources for this study include the Current Population Survey (CPS) March Supplement and Earnings File, NAWS, and the Census of Agriculture. Empirical support came from extensive research literature on hired farmworkers, including a previous Economic Research Service study that served as a baseline for elements of this report. CPS data allow for comparisons between hired farmworkers and workers in other occupations. This report used all other wage and salary workers as a reference group in order to compare the status of hired farmworkers relative to the total employed U.S. population (excluding farmworkers). In certain cases, hired farmworkers were compared with other occupations of similar skill levels.

Within each of the two groups consisting of farmworkers and other wage and salary employees as a group, CPS data also permit comparisons between workers with and without citizenship. Such comparisons are not equivalent to comparing authorized and unauthorized workers, but because legal status is such a critical socioeconomic characteristic, the citizen/noncitizen comparisons offer additional insight. NAWS data distinguished how hired crop farmworkers differ by unauthorized, authorized, and citizen legal status. Finally, data from the Census of Agriculture and the Agricultural Resource Management Survey place farm labor within the broader context of the agricultural sector.

INTRODUCTION

Hired farmworkers make up an estimated third of the total U.S. agricultural labor force and are critical to U.S. agricultural production, especially for labor-intensive agricultural sectors such as fruits and vegetables. A steadily increasing U.S. population, growing demand for labor-intensive crops, and a continually consolidating farm sector have stabilized the demand for hired farm labor in the past decade.

Changing geographic patterns of immigrant settlement in rural areas have increased the visibility of immigrants (Kandel and Cromartie, 2004). Changing production methods now permit year-round production for some farm enterprises, which has helped increasing numbers of formerly migratory workers settle permanently in nonmetropolitan counties.

The hired-farmworker labor market is unique in several respects:

1. Many farmworkers are mobile, traversing State and national boundaries. However, only an estimated 12 percent are "follow-the-crop" farmworkers who follow well-established migrant streams corresponding to agricultural production cycles.
2. Roughly half of all hired farmworkers in the United States lack legal authorization according to the U.S. Department of Labor, making their employment status tenuous and work circumstances and conditions more difficult.
3. Hired farmworkers face a challenging work environment that may include hazardous work conditions, low pay, and substandard housing conditions.

Consequently, while critical to many agricultural sectors, hired farmworkers remain among the most economically disadvantaged working groups in the United States. This relative position within the U.S. occupational structure has changed little over time (McWilliams, 1935; Griffith and Kissam, 1995). Safety improvements notwithstanding, agriculture remains one of the most hazardous industries in the Nation, and farmworkers encounter relatively unique risks from pesticides as well as conventional hazards from heavy equipment operation and physically strenuous labor (U.S. Department of Health and Human Services, 1998). Moreover, unauthorized workers fail to qualify for some social programs or choose not to use them for fear of deportation.

TOTAL ESTIMATES OF HIRED FARMWORKERS

In 2006, an average of 1.01 million hired farmworkers made up a third of the estimated 3 million people employed in agriculture. The other 2.05 million included self-employed farmers and their unpaid family members.[1] This report focuses exclusively on the characteristics and well-being of hired farmworkers. The 1.01 million figure is one of several cross-sectional estimates—ranging from 691,000 to as much as 1.4 million depending on the data source (see Appendix 2)—for the average number of hired farmworkers employed at any point throughout the year. Depending on the month or agricultural cycle, such estimates can change substantially. Moreover, high employment turnover means that an estimated 2.0 to 2.5 unique workers fill each farmworker job slot over the course of a year (Khan et al., 2003).

USDA's Farm Labor Survey remains the most accurate source of data on total counts of hired farmworkers. Other data sources and estimates yield different total counts of hired farmworkers (see Appendix 1), and each offers useful statistics on the characteristics and well-being of hired farmworkers. Current Population Survey (CPS) data, either from the 12-month Earnings File or the March Supplement, provide information on demographic and labor market characteristics and earnings. CPS data allow for comparisons between hired farmworkers and all wage and salary workers. Within each of these two employee subsets, CPS data also allow comparisons between workers with citizenship and those without. Such comparisons are not equivalent to comparing authorized and unauthorized workers, but because legal status is a critical socioeconomic characteristic, the citizen versus noncitizen comparison offers useful insights. The National Agricultural Workers Survey (NAWS) data provide more detailed information on legal status, but are limited to hired crop farmworkers and exclude hired livestock farmworkers. Census of Agriculture data and information from the Agricultural Resource Management Survey (ARMS) offer total labor costs per farm and information on farm structure.

---

[1] The 1.01 million figure is a rounded average of the four quarterly 2006 Farm Labor Report figures for hired farmworkers produced by the USDA's National Agricultural Statistics Service (NASS). This figure is comprised of two groups: farmworkers hired directly by farm operators (752,000) and agricultural service workers hired on a contract or fee basis (256,000) (see Glossary). The 3.06 million figure represents the sum of the 1.01 million figure plus a simple linear extrapolation to 2006 from the last available annual figures for self-employed and nonpaid family farmworkers collected by NASS from 2000 to 2002. NASS no longer collects data on this group of farmworkers, only hired farmworkers. Despite this limitation, we use the NASS data series because it provides historical context since 1950. See Appendixes 1 and 2 for more information on estimates of the total number of people employed in the agricultural sector.

FARM STRUCTURE AND LABOR DEMAND

Demand for hired farmworkers reflects structural changes in agricultural production and food consumption of an ever-growing U.S. and world population. Post World War II American agriculture has been characterized by increases in labor productivity, brought about through technological innovation (Dimitri et al., 2005; Fuglie et al., 2007). As a result, agricultural production now occurs on fewer and often larger farms. Data from the Census of Agriculture indicate that between 1950 and 2002 average farm size more than doubled, from 216 to 444 acres, while the total number of farms declined from to 5.5 to 2.1 million (Hoppe and Korb, 2005). Small farms, defined as those with sales of less than $250,000 annually, still account for over 90 percent of all farms, but produce less than 30 percent of all agricultural output.

Declining farm employment reflects these trends (figure 1). In 1950, the Census of Agriculture recorded almost 10 million people working on farms, including over 7.6 million farmers and their family members and 2.3 million hired farmworkers. Since that time, the number of family members and hired farmworkers has declined consistently to a total of just over 3 million in 2006. This corresponds to a drop in the proportion of the U.S. labor force employed in the agricultural sector from 12.5 percent in 1950 to less than 1.5 percent in 2006 (U.S. Census Bureau, 2007).

While declines in total farmworkers have leveled off since 1985, two unmistakable farm labor trends during the 20th century include a gradual decline in the use of labor inputs in general, and, for labor inputs used, a growing reliance on nonfamily hired farm labor (figure 2). From 1950 to 2006, according to the Farm Labor Survey (FLS), the average number of family farmworkers per farm declined 27 percent, from 1.35 to 0.98, while the average number of hired farmworkers per farm increased from 0.41 to 0.59, between 1950 and 1985, before declining to 0.48 in 2006. As a consequence, the ratio of hired farmworkers to total farmworkers has increased from roughly 1 in 4 in 1950 to 1 in 3 in 2006. Moreover, because the FLS is a cross-section estimate at various points during the year and hired farmworkers are often seasonal workers, notwithstanding the recent increase in year-round workers, the total number of hired farmworkers over the course of a year is likely to be significantly higher than the FLS estimates.

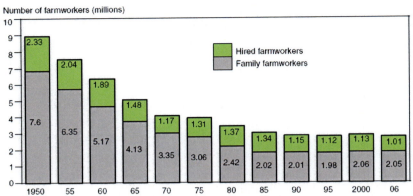

Notes: Family farmworkers include self-employed farmers and unpaid family members. Hired farmworkers include direct hires and agricultural service workers who are often hired through labor contractors. The 2006 family farmworkers figure of 2.05 million is estimated from a simple linear extrapolation from the last available annual figures for self-employed and nonpaid family farmworkers collected by NASS from 2000 to 2002.

Source: Farm Labor Survey, National Agricultural Statistics Service, USDA.

Figure 1. Total family and hired farmworkers on U.S. farms, 1950-2006.

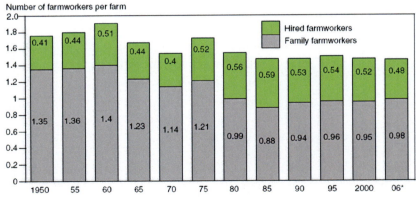

* Based on linear projection of earlier trends.

Notes: Family farmworkers include self-employed farmers and unpaid family members. Hired farmworkers include direct hires and agricultural service workers who are often hired through labor contractors.

Source: Farm Labor Survey, National Agricultural Statistics Service, USDA.

Figure 2. Average number of family and hired farmworkers per farm, 1950-2006.

Labor occupies a prominent place as the third largest production expense (considering all cash and noncash expenses, such as capital depreciation), behind feed and capital depreciation for the agricultural sector as a whole (figure 3). For 2007, employee compensation for hired labor is forecast to be $22.8 billion. After declining for decades, labor's share of U.S. farm expenses began increasing in the mid-1980s. Consequently, any factors affecting the farm labor supply—such as minimum wage increases, changes in labor demand from other industries employing low-skilled workers (e.g., construction, manufacturing), or new immigration policies—will alter farm profitability and viability among agricultural sectors heavily reliant on farm labor. Growers who specialize in vegetables, fruits and nuts, and horticultural products, for which labor costs range from 30 to 40 percent of total expenses, are especially sensitive to fluctuations in the cost and availability of labor.

Growing reliance on foreign-born, hired farmworkers became firmly institutionalized at the outset of World War II with the Bracero Program, an immigration-related farm labor policy that allowed agricultural growers to hire Mexican workers to make up for war-induced labor shortfalls. This program lasted 22 years, from 1942 until 1964, when several factors including public concern over abusive labor practices, the rising use of unauthorized labor, and the growing farm labor movement convinced Congress to terminate it (Martin, 2003; Massey et al., 2002). During the Bracero Program and following its demise, unauthorized immigration to the United States grew, becoming an established trend by the 1980s. The Immigration Reform and Control Act of 1986 (IRCA), which was intended to reduce unauthorized immigration, regularized the legal status of over 1 million hired farmworkers between 1986 and 1989, but also increased penalties to employers who hired unauthorized workers. Nevertheless, after a brief respite, unauthorized immigration increased and continues to occur in substantial numbers.

Agricultural producers have become accustomed to having a large pool of hired farmworkers available, and they continue to utilize a largely immigrant workforce that includes many who lack authorization to work in the United States. Despite increased border and employer enforcement policies, close to half of all farmworkers are unauthorized. While agricultural tasks for some crops have been automated, some growers contend that the expense of mechanization for other, currently labor-intensive products such as tree fruit and horticulture would prevent them from remaining competitive with foreign producers (American Farm Bureau Federation, 2006). Other research suggests that growers could adjust to smaller workforces with labor-efficient technologies and management practices (Martin, 2007). Both arguments remain untested because growers have relied upon a relatively ample labor supply (Levine, 2007).

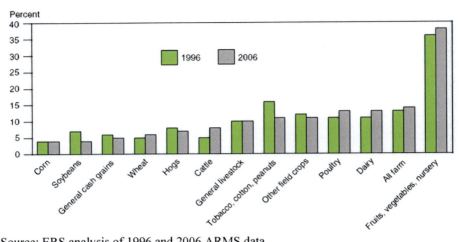

Source: ERS analysis of 1996 and 2006 ARMS data.

Figure 3. Labor's share of total cash expenses, by agricultural product, 1996 and 2006.

GEOGRAPHY OF FARM LABOR

The geographic distribution of the hired farm labor force reflects the total quantity of agricultural production and the kind of crops grown in an area (figure 4). Certain crops are more labor intensive. One way to put this in context is to compare labor expenses to cash receipts. For the United States, the total farm labor expense in 2006 was $24.4 billion—amounting to 10.2 percent of total agricultural commodity cash receipts. But, in California, which has the highest cash receipts of any State and produces many labor-intensive products (such as dairy, grapes, and greenhouse/nursery), total farm labor expense amounted to 22.3 percent of the total value of agricultural cash receipts for 2006. In contrast, in Iowa, farm labor expense totaled 2.5 percent of cash receipts. Iowa has the third highest total cash receipts, but grows primarily non-labor-intensive agricultural commodities (such as corn, hogs, and soybeans).

Since 1980, the geographic distribution of farmworkers has shifted, with proportions declining in both the South and Midwest and increasing in the West and Southwest. Roughly 60 percent of all hired farmworkers currently work in crops and 40 percent work in livestock. Most hired crop farmworkers are located disproportionately in the Southwest, with California and Texas accounting for almost a third of the $22 billion spent on hired farm and contract farm labor expenses in the United States in 2002 (figure 5).

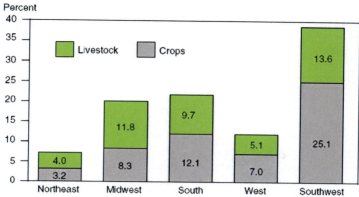

Notes: The sum of all figures equals 100 percent. We altered the four standard Census regions (Northeast, Midwest, South, and West) by identifying a 5-state Southwest region, extracted from the West and South regions, that includes Arizona, California, Colorado, New Mexico, and Texas (see Glossary). The percentages of farmworkers in each geographic region from the 2006 CPS Earnings File in this chart match, within 1 percent, the same geographic distribution of farm labor expenses found in the 2002 Census of Agriculture.

Source: ERS analysis of annual averages from 2006 Current Population Survey Earnings.

Figure 4. Hired farmworkers by geographic region and product type, 2006.

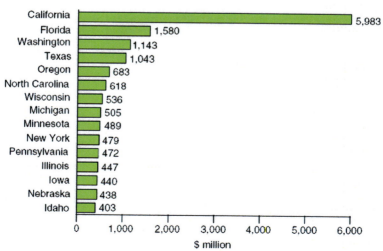

Source: ERS analysis of 2002 Census of Agriculture data.

Figure 5. Top 15 States for hired farm and contract farm labor expenses, 2002.

Demographic Characteristics

The demographic profile of hired farmworkers contributes to their economic disadvantage relative to most other wage and salary workers in the United States (table 1). On average, they are younger, less educated, more likely to be foreign-born, and less likely to be citizens or authorized to work in the United States. The extent of this disadvantage depends on which data are used to represent the hired-farmworker population (Larson et al., 2002). We used CPS data to compare hired farmworkers with all wage and salary workers, but these data reflect characteristics of more established residents willing to respond to formal, repeated home-based interviews. To obtain an additional measure of relative disadvantage among unauthorized farm- workers, we present figures for each group by citizenship status. Presenting characteristics by citizenship status is not equivalent to presenting them by legal status, because many noncitizens possess legal authorization to work in the United States. Nevertheless, given the lack of complete legal status information, citizenship status roughly approximates the degree to which differences in authorized versus unauthorized status differentiate the farmworker population.

Hired farmworkers differ from other wage and salary workers, as a group, due to the gender imbalance of the hired farm workforce. Obstacles to international migration and the close living and working conditions of most U.S. farmworkers often present difficult or untenable circumstances for potential female migrants and their families. Hence, most hired farmworkers are men. Approximately 1 of every 5 hired farmworkers is female, compared with gender parity found among wage and salary workers in general.

Farm labor is physically demanding, and hired farmworkers tend to be younger than other wage and salary workers, in general. Visible differences between these two groups appear at the ends of the age distribution: the proportion of farmworkers in the youngest age group exceeds that of wage and salary workers in general, while the proportion in the oldest age group trails that of other wage and salary workers. Despite youth and gender imbalance, over half of all farmworkers are married, and in this respect they closely resemble all wage and salary workers (see box, "Children in Agricultural Labor").

The racial and ethnic makeup of the hired farm labor force has changed significantly in recent decades, the most consequential transformation being the increasing proportion of Hispanic farmworkers.[2] According to 2006 CPS data, 43

---

[2] "Hispanic" is a pan-ethnic term that encompasses people whose origins include Mexico, Central America, South America, and the Caribbean. People who self-identify as Hispanic or

percent of all hired farmworkers are Hispanic: for hired crop and hired livestock workers, the figures are 56 and 26 percent Hispanic, respectively (data not shown). Almost all noncitizen farmworkers are Hispanic. Yet, since noncitizens comprise only about a third of all farmworkers, the total CPS figure of 43 percent continues to differ substantially from the 2006 NAWS figure of over 80 percent for hired crop farmworkers. Survey methodology explains the discrepancy between these two national data sets. CPS data are collected from households each month over a 16-month period and, therefore, reflect characteristics of more established residents. NAWS data, on the other hand, are collected at the worksite and are therefore more likely to capture persons who have less stable living arrangements and who tend to avoid participation in more formal data collection efforts (Mehta et al., 2000).

Table 1. Demographic characteristics of hired farmworkers and all wage and salary workers as a group, by citizenship status, 2006

	Hired farmworkers			Wage & salary workers		
	Noncitizen	Citizen	Total	Noncitizen	Citizen	Total
			Percent			
Citizenship status	37.6	62.4	100.0	9.2	90.8	100.0
Sex						
Male	82.7	79.9	80.9	63.6	50.7	52.1
Female	17.3	20.1	19.1	36.4	49.3	47.9
Median age (years)	34	34	34	34	40	40
Age distribution						
Between ages 15-21	4.2	21.7	15.1	4.9	7.0	6.9
Between ages 21-44	74.0	46.4	56.4	72.9	52.9	54.7
Over age 44	21.8	31.9	28.1	22.3	40.1	38.4
Hispanic ethnicity	94.6	12.0	43.0	61.8	9.1	13.7
Race						
White	94.3	90.2	91.7	73.4	82.4	81.6
Black	0.6	6.0	4.0	8.3	12.4	11.9

Latino may be of any race. Hispanic farm- workers in the CPS are overwhelmingly of Mexican origin (94.5 percent) and Central and South American origin (3.4 percent). According to the CPS data, 84 percent of Hispanic hired farmworkers were born in Mexico. In contrast, 94 percent of non-Hispanic hired farm- workers were born in the United States.

Table 1. (Continued).

	Hired farmworkers			Wage & salary workers		
	Noncitizen	Citizen	Total	Noncitizen	Citizen	Total
			Percent			
Native American	2.1	1.0	1.4	0.9	0.7	0.7
Asian	3.0	2.9	2.9	17.5	4.6	5.7
Educational attainment						
Less than 9th grade	63.4	9.9	30.0	22.2	1.4	3.5
9-12 yrs, no diploma	15.4	24.5	21.1	15.6	7.8	8.6
High school graduate	15.9	35.7	28.2	26.2	30.0	29.6
Some college	5.4	30.0	20.7	36.0	60.8	58.3
Country of birth						
Mexico	90.3	5.3	37.3	41.2	1.2	5.1
All other countries	9.7	2.0	4.9	58.8	6.6	11.3
United States	0.0	92.6	57.8	0.0	92.2	83.6
Year entered U.S. (for foreign born)						
Before 1986	17.5	72.5	23.5	15.7	60.4	35.5
1986-1995	29.2	21.1	28.3	29.6	28.6	29.1
1996-2005	53.3	6.4	48.2	54.7	11.0	35.3
Spanish only household	64.0	4.1	26.7	30.7	1.3	4.0
Marital status						
Married	62.5	46.9	52.7	60.3	55.3	55.7
Divi widi sep.	8.2	9.7	9.1	8.9	15.3	14.7
Never married	29.3	43.4	38.1	30.8	29.4	29.6
Children under 18 in household	46.7	29.2	35.8	42.4	34.5	35.2

Source: ERS analysis of annual averages from 2006 Current Population Survey Earnings File data.

Hispanic ethnicity is particularly important. Because of the large proportion of foreign-born Hispanic farmworkers, many of whom originate from poor rural Latin American communities, measuring Hispanic ethnicity is critical for accurately profiling this workforce. NAWS data illustrate how hired crop farmworkers increasingly originate from Mexico, a trend that became especially pronounced during the 1990s when a growing service sector created plentiful alternatives to farm labor employment for low-skilled, native-born workers (figure 6).

Other racial and ethnic changes also merit attention. Data from the 1987 CPS (not shown) indicate that non-Hispanic Blacks, mostly in the South, made up 8 percent of the hired-farmworker population (Oliveira and Cox, 1990). That figure has since declined to 4 percent (table 1). The small Native American and Asian populations of hired farmworkers did not change significantly in 2006.

The education gap between Hispanics and non-Hispanics is due largely to the high proportion of recently arrived, foreign-born Hispanics, many of whom originate from rural communities with limited education and work opportunities. The average educational attainment in such communities is 9 years of education, the equivalent of U.S. middle school. The education gap is particularly pronounced for "entry-level" occupations, like farmwork, which attract the newest immigrants. It becomes less pronounced and occurs farther down the education continuum for all wage and salary workers who include large proportions of native-born Hispanics (figure 7). Results displayed by Hispanic ethnicity closely resemble those by citizenship status (table 1).

Children in Agricultural Labor

The youth portion of the farm labor force is notable. NAWS data indicate that between 1989 and 2006, on average, children under age 18 made up 5.5 percent of the hired crop farmworker labor force. These children were equally divided by gender as well as by legal status. NAWS data indicate fluctuations in the proportion of child farmworkers and an overall decline since 1995.

Farmwork provides opportunities for young people to earn money while in school or during the summer, and children under age 18 often work on their parents' farms. The median weeks per year worked by children (11.1) is about a third that of adults (29.9), according to NAWS data for 1989-2006. Nevertheless, several studies indicate a lack of safeguards to fully protect children (Edid, 1994; Rothenberg, 1998; NIOSH, 2003).

In several comprehensive reports, the U.S. Government Accountability Office (GAO, 1998; 2002) detailed the prevalence of agricultural child labor legislative protections and their enforcement, and Federal educational assistance programs for children in migrant and seasonal agriculture.

The GAO reports raise several concerns, including lack of accurate head counts due to incomplete data; lack of legal protections for children working in agriculture compared with other industries; lack of labor regulation enforcement; and lack of information to assess the effectiveness of education and labor programs for children in agriculture.

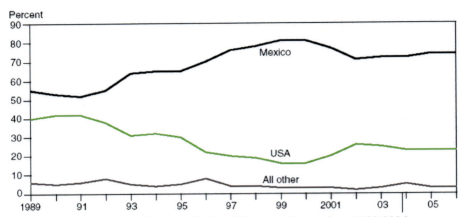

Source: ERS analysis of National Agricultural Workers Survey data, 1989-2006

Figure 6. Nationality of crop farmworker population, 1989-2006.

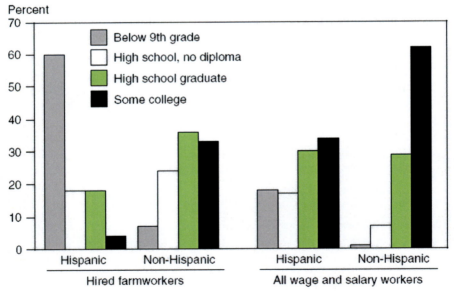

Source: ERS analysis of annual averages from 2006 Current Population Survey Earnings File data.

Figure 7. Educational attainment by Hispanic ethnicity, 2006.

LEGAL STATUS

Legal status influences economic and social well-being through its impact on outcomes ranging from social service eligibility, employment, residential mobility, working conditions, and wages (Isé and Perloff, 1995; RiveraBatiz, 1999; Kossoudji and Cobb-Clark, 2000). Legal status is a perpetual concern for farmworkers and growers alike. For farmworkers, unauthorized status means facing a greater likelihood of unfair labor practices and deportation (Rothenberg, 1998; Martin, 2003). Growers, in turn, are concerned about having sufficient numbers of workers during critical work periods as well as complying with Federal and State administrative requirements to ensure workers are authorized to work in the United States.

While CPS data do not distinguish between authorized and unauthorized status among those lacking U.S. citizenship, they provide some sense of relative scale. Roughly 40 percent of all hired farmworkers are noncitizens compared with 10 percent of all wage and salary workers. The NAWS contacts a higher proportion of unauthorized workers than the CPS and distinguishes their status from legally authorized workers or citizens (figure 8). According to NAWS data for 2004-2006, roughly 50 percent of all hired crop farmworkers lacked authorized status. This higher rate also reflects a higher proportion of Hispanic workers in the NAWS than in the CPS.

Like most unauthorized immigrants, unauthorized farmworkers rely on changes in U.S. immigration policies for opportunities to obtain legal status. For instance, the Immigration Reform and Control Act (IRCA), which included the Special Agricultural Worker (SAW) legalization provision, regularized the status of over 1 million unauthorized farmworkers at the end of the 1980s (Massey et al., 2002). Applicants who could prove they had worked in the United States between 1985 and 1986 were granted legal status. Since then, however, unauthorized farmworkers have not been offered special provisions to obtain legal status, and the majority who entered since 1990 remain unauthorized (figure 9) (see box, "The H-2A Visa Program for Temporary Agricultural Workers").

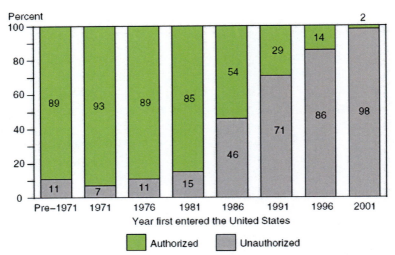

Note: The three most current years of data are used to increase the precision of these estimates by reflecting the most recently surveyed hired crop farmworkers.
Source: ERS analysis of National Agricultural Workers Survey data, 2004-2006.

Figure 8. Legal compostion of recent hired crop farmworkers, by year of entry into the United States.

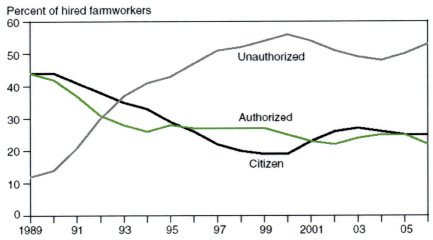

Source: ERS analysis of National Agricultural Workers Survey data, 1989-2006.

Figure 9. Legal status of hired crop farmworkers, 1989-2006.

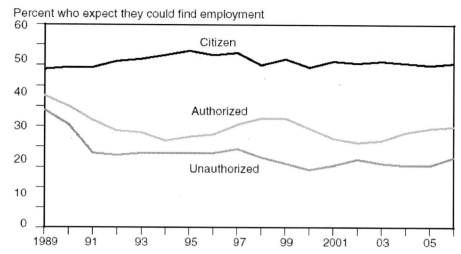

Note: Values are averaged over 3 years to smooth fluctuations.
Source: ERS analysis of National Agricultural Workers Survey data, 1989-2006.

Figure 10. Hired crop farmworkers' expectations of obtaining nonfarm U.S. employment within a month, by legal status, 1989-2006.

The unauthorized proportion of foreign-born workers tends to be higher in agriculture than in other industries because agriculture has served as a point-of-entry into the U.S. labor market for unauthorized immigrants. A review of hired crop farmworker legal status from the end of IRCA's legalization provisions in 1989 to the present shows that as the older cohorts of farmworkers cycle out of agriculture and obtain jobs in other industries, the remaining workers are recent arrivals who lack legal status.

Unauthorized workers have fewer avenues for economic mobility outside of agricultural work, and their own perceptions of the U.S. labor market reflect these circumstances (figure 10). Initially, after IRCA, 58 percent of all unauthorized hired crop farmworkers felt they could obtain a nonfarm job within a month, a proportion 7 percentage points lower than that of authorized workers. By 2006, the gap between the two groups had widened to 15 percentage points despite a recent upsurge in both groups' expectations.

While trend-lines fluctuated similarly for both groups from 1989 to 2006, the diverging outcomes indicate a growing rift of economic prospects between those with authorized legal status and those without it.

The H-2A Visa Program for Temporary Agricultural Workers

The H-2A visa program, operated cooperatively by the U.S. Department of Labor (DOL) and the U.S. Citizenship and Immigration Services Division of the Department of Homeland Security (DHS), processed over 64,000 agricultural worker applications in 2006 (DOL, 2007). This class of nonimmigrant admission that originated in 1943 was converted into a specific Federal legal provision in 1952, revised by IRCA, and amended by subsequent legislation. It permits employers to hire temporary foreign-born workers for up to 1 year with possible extensions for up to 3 years. H-2A visa holders are considered nonimmigrants because they are admitted temporarily to perform work; immigrants by contrast are admitted to the United States as legal permanent residents.

To hire these workers, employers must demonstrate they lack a sufficient and timely supply of locally available qualified U.S. workers, and that using foreign workers would not adversely affect wages and working conditions of comparably employed U.S. workers. H-2A workers must earn the higher of the prevailing industry wage, the Federal or State minimum wage, or an Adverse Effect Wage Rate (AEWR) which is an average hourly wage rate based on data collected by USDA, and employers must provide them with detailed earnings statements when paid.

Employers are required to provide H-2A workers with a series of benefits, including housing that meets Federal standards for noncommuting workers, transportation for commuting workers, transportation to workers' home countries or next employment locations, either food preparation facilities or three meals per day, and workers' compensation insurance. U.S. workers must be offered the same benefits as H-2A workers.

Employers must apply to the DOL and their State Workforce Agency 45 days prior to hiring. After employers have met certain working condition stipulations, the DOL "certifies" within 7 days that there are not enough U.S. workers to fill these positions through State and employer recruitment during this period and that the presence of H-2A workers will not adversely affect local wages. Once filed, over 90 percent of employer applications are approved for most of the jobs requested. Following successful certification, the employer next petitions the Citizenship and Immigration Services Division of DHS.

Approved petitions are sent to the appropriate consulates where workers apply for visas. At the port of entry, a Customs and Border Protection officer authorizes a traveler's admission into the United States and the period of time that the individual bearer of the nonimmigrant visa is allowed to remain in the United States for that visit.

Although less than 5 percent of all hired farmworkers are hired through the program, it remains controversial. Obstacles for farm operators wishing to use the H-2A visa program include:

- Complicated paperwork;
- Requirements to try domestic worker recruitment before utilizing the program;
- Requirements to anticipate future labor demand;
- The requirement to pay the higher of the prevailing industry wage, the Federal or State minimum wage, or the AEWR; and
- Unwanted attention from advocacy groups and unions reviewing publicly accessible H-2A requests.

Farmworker advocates and unions have also been critical of the program, arguing that it lacks fundamental protections to prevent foreign workers from being mistreated and exploited (GAO, 1997; Griffith, 2006; Southern Poverty Law Center, 2007). At the time this report was written, Congress was considering the Agricultural Job Opportunities, Benefits and Security Act legislation known as AgJobs that includes three major changes to the H-2A program. These include:

1. Allowing farmers to assert, rather than certify, that they have unfilled worker positions;
2. Allowing farmers to pay a housing allowance rather than provide actual housing; and
3. Eliminating or freezing the AEWR (Martin, 2007).

EMPLOYMENT

In addition to describing populations, demographic characteristics effectively predict economic outcomes. Age, educational attainment, employment experience, English language ability, and legal status all strongly influence earnings and occupational mobility. The disadvantaged demographic profile described earlier for hired farmworkers relative to all wage and salary workers in the U.S. labor force often translates into less favorable employment characteristics (table 2).

Farmworkers typically have more gaps in employment than nonfarm wage and salary workers and fewer opportunities to earn additional compensation. They are twice as likely to have schedules that either vary or exceed 50 hours per week, corresponding to sudden requirements of agricultural production. Yet among farmworkers, noncitizens are more likely to be employed 40 hours per week and less likely to have more flexible or more demanding work schedules. Noncitizen farmworkers are also more likely to be employed full-time. Part-time farmworkers who are citizens have a median age (18) that is half that of noncitizen part-time farmworkers (37), suggesting a greater presence of high-school or college-age workers among part-time workers with citizenship.

Table 2. Select employment characteristics of hired farmworkers and all other wage and salary workers as a group, by citizenship status, 2006

	Hired farmworkers			Wage and salary workers		
Noncitizen		Citizen	Total	Noncitizen	Citizen	Total
Hours worked prior week			*Percent*			
Hours vary	13.6	22.0	18.8	7.1	8.1	8.0
Less than 35 hours	5.4	18.6	13.6	10.6	14.9	14.5
Between 40-50 hours	70.7	41.0	52.2	76.7	69.5	70.1
More than 50 hours	10.3	18.4	15.4	5.6	7.6	7.4
Employment status						
Full-time	93.7	75.0	82.4	88.1	83.0	83.5
Part-time	6.3	25.0	17.6	11.9	17.0	16.5
Salary status[1]						
Hourly wage worker	75.9	55.7	63.1	68.3	58.8	59.7
Nonhourly worker[1]	24.1	44.3	36.9	31.7	41.2	40.3
Have more than one job	0.3	7.1	4.5	2.9	5.6	5.3
Receive overtime pay, tips, commissions	7.0	5.1	5.8	9.9	14.9	14.3
Union membership	1.7	2.2	2.0	6.3	12.6	12.0

[1] For wage and salary workers, nonhourly worker status usually refers to salaries. For hired farm- workers, it refers to both salaries and piece-rate earnings. The latter are often significantly lower. Source: ERS analysis of annual averages from 2006 Current Population Survey Earnings File data.

Farmworkers are about as likely as other wage and salary workers to earn hourly wages and, despite low earnings, are also about as likely to have only one job at any given time. Yet, because of the seasonal nature of farmwork, they are more likely to have a succession of jobs over a given time period. Hired farmworkers are less likely to earn overtime pay, tips, or commissions, or to join labor unions. NAWS data (not shown) also indicate a low proportion of union coverage for hired farmworkers.

CPS data indicate that when farmworkers are employed, they have relatively stable work schedules. However, due to the seasonal nature of their work, hired farmworkers, on average, experience rates of unemployment double those of wage and salary workers, in general, a difference that varies by demographic and economic characteristics (table 3). For instance, the unemployment rate of female farmworkers exceeds by threefold that of all female wage and salary workers. This relative disadvantage also accrues to workers who are over age 44, Hispanic, noncitizen, and foreign-born. Farmworkers with at least 9 years of schooling, on the other hand, experience unemployment rates that are comparable to those of all wage and salary workers. A number of these characteristics overlap. Recent international migrants, who are also likely to be younger, Hispanic, less educated, and unauthorized, face the greatest challenges obtaining employment.

Among hired farmworkers, unemployment rates also vary by sector and occupation. Those working in field crops have average unemployment rates more than quadruple those of livestock workers, owing to the more seasonal nature of field crop work. Nonsupervisory farmworkers have 2.5 times the unemployment rate of managers and supervisors.

Unemployment characteristics also reflect greater employment instability over the course of a year (table 4). Hired farmworkers are more likely to have terminated employment due to layoffs or the conclusion of a temporary job and less likely to have quit or previously been employed full-time prior to searching for work.

Lower unemployment durations of farmworkers reflect several factors, including low barriers to entry for farm labor and the inability of hired farmworkers to remain unemployed for extended periods. Longer unemployment spells among hired farmworkers, many of whom are foreign-born, increase the chance that some of these workers will return to their countries of origin. When that occurs, such workers effectively remove themselves from the pool of potential survey respondents and, consequently, any and all resulting official statistics.

The unemployment rate for hired farmworkers (figure 11) was among the highest for all major occupations in 2006 and stems mainly from farmwork's seasonality. When employed, hired farmworkers work for roughly the same number of hours per week as other workers, yet total employment levels for hired farmworkers vary according to season. For example, NASS data for 2006 indicate that 1,195,000 hired farmworkers were employed in mid-July, compared with 796,000 in mid-January.

Hired farmworkers have historically earned relatively low wages (Griffith and Kissam, 1995; Rothenberg, 1998; Martin, 2003; Martin et al., 2006).

Table 3. Unemployment rate by economic and demographic characteristics of hired farmworkers and all wage and salary workers, by citizenship status, 2006

	Hired farmworkers			Wage and salary workers		
	Noncitizen	Citizen	Total	Noncitizen	Citizen	Total
	Percent					
All workers	9.9	7.7	8.5	4.3	4.5	4.5
Sex						
Female	17.6	11.6	13.7	5.1	4.3	4.4
Male	8.1	6.6	7.2	3.8	4.7	4.6
Age distribution						
Between ages 15-21	14.3	10.8	11.2	7.0	9.7	9.6
Between ages 21-44	8.3	8.8	8.3	4.0	4.8	4.7
Over age 44	14.3	4.5	7.6	4.6	3.2	3.3
Hispanic ethnicity						
Hispanic	9.5	15.0	10.5	4.4	4.9	4.8
Non-Hispanic	17.3	6.6	7.0	4.1	4.5	4.5
Race						
White	9.6	7.5	8.3	4.3	3.9	4.0
Black	I/C	9.8	10.9	6.1	8.3	8.1
Native American	0.0	13.0	6.1	5.8	8.0	7.7
Asian	21.5	7.6	13.6	3.2	3.6	3.5
Educational attainment						
Less than 9th grade	12.0	11.7	12.0	5.1	5.7	5.7
9-12 years, no diploma	9.6	9.3	9.4	5.6	10.1	9.4
High school graduate	4.2	7.5	6.8	4.0	5.6	5.5
Some college	0.5	5.1	4.7	3.3	3.2	3.2
Year entered U.S. (for foreign-born)						
Before 1986	13.3	10.3	12.3	4.9	3.0	3.6
1986-1995	13.0	11.2	12.8	4.3	3.2	4.0
1996-2005	7.0	5.4	6.9	4.1	4.0	4.1
Marital status						
Married	8.5	5.0	6.6	3.9	2.7	2.8

Div/wid/sep.	11.3	9.3	10.0	5.1	5.2	5.2
Never married	12.4	10.1	10.7	4.8	7.4	7.1
Industrial sector						
Crops	12.8	12.1	12.4	N/A	N/A	N/A
Livestock	1.1	3.7	3.1	N/A	N/A	N/A
Occupation						
Farmworkers	10.5	8.6	9.4	N/A	N/A	N/A
Managers/supervisors	2.1	4.1	3.7	N/A	N/A	N/A

Notes: N/A – not applicable. I/C – insufficient cases.
Source: ERS analysis of annual averages from 2006 Current Population Survey Earnings File data.

Table 4. Reasons for unemployment and duration of unemployment, 2006

	Hired farmworkers			Wage and salary workers		
	Noncitizen	Citizen	Total	Noncitizen	Citizen	Total
	Percent					
Reasons for unemployment						
Lost job—laid off	47.2	32.3	38.9	17.0	14.0	14.5
Lost job—other reason	1.3	12.8	7.7	25.0	27.3	26.9
Temporary job ended	31.4	17.5	23.7	13.8	10.0	10.5
Quit	3.4	2.4	2.9	9.9	13.6	13.2
Job re-entrants[1]	16.7	35.0	26.9	34.3	35.1	34.9
Total	100.0	100.0	100.0	100.0	100.0	100.0
Duration of unemployment						
0-3 months	27.9	36.5	32.7	30.1	25.5	26.0
4-6 months	18.4	20.2	19.4	17.7	17.3	17.4
7-12 months	19.0	13.9	16.2	20.7	21.3	21.2
13+ months	34.6	29.4	31.7	31.6	35.9	35.5
Total	100.0	100.0	100.0	100.0	100.0	100.0
Median (months)	8	4	6	7	8	8

[1]"People who previously worked at a full-time job lasting 2 weeks or longer, but are out of the labor force prior to beginning to look for work" (U.S. Department of Commerce, 2005). Source: ERS analysis of annual averages from 2006 Current Population Survey Earnings File data.

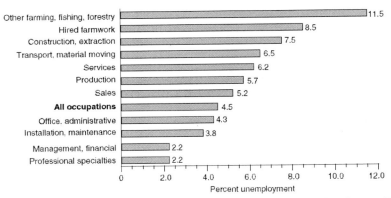

Source: ERS analysis of annual averages from 2006 Current Population Survey Earnings File data.

Figure 11. Unemployment rates by occupation, 2006.

According to CPS data, median weekly earnings of full-time farmworkers are 59 percent of those for all wage and salary workers (table 5). The earnings gap between the two groups is smaller in the Midwest where farmworker earnings exceed the national farmworker median. The gap is greater for farmworkers in the Northeast whose earnings trail the national farmworker median, while those of all wage and salary workers exceed the national median. Within the farmworker population, supervisory and managerial personnel earn 57 percent more than nonsupervisory workers, and livestock workers, who often have more stable employment, earn roughly 24 percent more than crop workers.[3]

Over time, wages and earnings of hired farmworkers vary as immigration policies tighten or loosen the labor supply (figure 12). Between the end of the Bracero Program in 1964 and passage of IRCA in 1986, unauthorized migration steadily increased and hired farmworker real wages either stabilized or dropped in response (Massey et al., 2002). Following IRCA, real wages increased only slightly until increased border enforcement policies in the mid-1990s restricted the flow of unauthorized workers. Average real wages increased 10 percent between 1995 and

---

[3] Reconciling the national agricultural labor expenditure reported in the ARMS and that based on median weekly earnings reported in the Current Population Survey multiplied by the total number of farmworkers is complicated by several issues. Farmers reporting their labor expenses in the ARMS include payroll taxes not paid to workers and contract labor expense. In addition, published reports using ARMS data often report labor expenses that include a measure of the opportunity costs of unpaid/family farmworkers. Removing these supplemental expenses yields a figure that coincides with the weekly earnings figures reported in this report from the Current Population Survey Earnings File data.

2000. Since the events of 9/11, real wages have continued to increase as the number of hired farmworkers declined. Hired-farmworker hourly wages, which are measured in NASS's Farm Labor Survey, the CPS, and the NAWS, would be substantially higher if they did not include a large proportion of unauthorized workers whose average wages are lower than those of authorized workers.

Table 5. Median weekly earnings by employment characteristic for full-time hired farmworkers, by citizenship status, 2006

		Hired farmworkers			Wage and salary workers		
		Noncitizen	Citizen	Total	Noncitizen	Citizen	Total
				Dollars			
All workers		340	470	400	480	700	673
Industrial sector							
Crops		318	462	360	N/A	N/A	N/A
Livestock		400	480	448	N/A	N/A	N/A
Occupation							
Farmworkers		338	440	382	N/A	N/A	N/A
Managers/supervisors		408	625	598	N/A	N/A	N/A
Full-time status							
Full-time		340	470	400	480	700	673
Part-time		270	150	150	213	204	204
Geographic region							
Northeast		280	475	420	538	769	750
Midwest		384	525	500	500	692	680
South		320	433	385	470	654	635
West		353	462	390	480	704	686
Southwest		350	466	384	440	731	673
Hourly wage							
Median		7.50	10.00	8.00	10.00	13.00	13.00
Mean		7.84	10.43	8.95	11.95	15.25	14.82

Note: N/A – not applicable.
Source: ERS analysis of annual averages from 2006 Current Population Survey Earnings File data.

Hired farmworkers not only earn less, on average, than wage and salary workers as a group, but crop farmworkers also earn less than workers in similar low-skill occupations (figure 13). Wages remain low in spite of the fact that labor analysts consider farmwork among the most arduous and hazardous occupations. Factors accounting for the relatively low earnings of farmworkers, include: a high proportion of unauthorized workers who have fewer options to seek employment in other industries; the use of farm labor contractors who reduce the hourly pay of hired farmworkers in exchange for arranging employment with growers; and, in the case of small farms, exemption from Federal minimum wage laws.

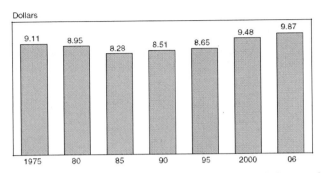

Notes: Figures reflect wages paid to hired crop and hired livestock farmworkers, as well as supervisory and nonsupervisory workers. Nominal dollars were converted to real dollars using the Consumer Price Index (CPI).
Source: National Agriculture Statistics Service, USDA.

Figure 12. Real hourly wages (2005) for all hired farmworkers, 1975-2006.

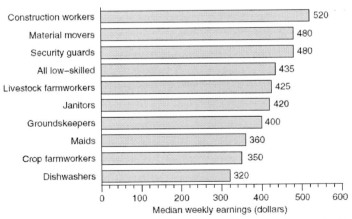

Note: Weekly earnings include wages, bonuses, overtime pay, tips, and other forms of monetary compensation.
Source: ERS analysis of annual averages from 2006 Current Population Survey Earnings File data.

Figure 13. Median weekly earnings across select low-skill occupations, 2006.

Demographic characteristics also influence hired-farmworker earnings and their relative difference compared to earnings of other wage and salary workers (table 6). The earnings gap shrinks for people who are similarly disadvantaged, namely the youngest, least-educated, and unauthorized workers. Otherwise, the average earnings gap does not vary substantially across most demographic characteristics. Based on the characteristics of race and ethnicity, Hispanics incur the smallest wage differences and Asians the largest for farm versus nonfarm employment.

Another way to compare hired-farmworker earnings with the rest of the U.S. labor force is to place them in the context of an earnings distribution (figure 14). The range of earnings for all wage and salary employees, divided into 10 even deciles, serves as the baseline for this comparison. If the distribution of hired-farmworkers' earnings is then superimposed over that of all wage and salary workers, we can see that while supervisory farmworker earnings roughly mimic those of all wage and salary workers, nonsupervisory farm- worker earnings concentrate at the lower end, with over 80 percent falling within the first four deciles of the U.S. workforce.

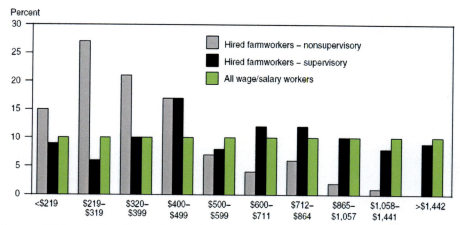

Source: ERS analysis of annual averages from 2006 Current Population Survey Earnings File data.

Figure 14. Distribution of hired farmworkers and all wage and salary workers, by average weekly earnings decile.

Table 6. Median weekly earnings, by demographic characteristic for full-time hired farmworkers, by citizenship status, 2006

	Hired			Wage and salary workers			
	Noncitizen	Citizen	Total	Noncitizen	Citizen	Total	
	Dollars						
All workers	340	470	448	480	700	788	0.57
Sex							
Female	290	420	350	420	613	600	0.58
Male	350	480	400	490	794	750	0.53
Age distribution							
Between ages 15-21	280	350	312	340	355	350	0.89
Between ages 21-44	340	480	400	480	673	640	0.63
Over age 44	360	481	442	500	783	769	0.57
Hispanic ethnicity							
Hispanic	340	414	350	400	576	480	0.73
Non-Hispanic	360	481	475	680	720	720	0.66
Race							
White	340	485	400	440	728	692	0.58
Black	I/C	360	360	480	568	560	0.64
Native American	330	385	330	420	557	531	0.62
Asian	400	413	400	748	769	760	0.53
Marital status							
Married	350	500	404	500	784	760	0.53
Div./wid./sep.	338	542	438	450	670	650	0.67
Never married	320	400	369	415	560	538	0.69
Educational attainment							
Less than 9th grade	336	322	336	394	440	400	0.84
9-12 years, no dipl.	350	440	400	400	425	406	0.99
High school grad	384	500	462	450	577	560	0.83
Some college	350	560	500	750	823	808	0.62
Country of birth							
Mexico	340	430	350	400	520	405	0.86
All other countries	350	507	360	560	748	646	0.56
United States	N/A	475	475	N/A	700	700	0.68
Year entered U.S. (for foreign-born)							
Before 1986	346	432	360	506	730	673	0.53
1986-1995	350	485	350	480	650	543	0.64
1996-2006	336	I/C	338	460	537	480	0.70

Note: N/A= not applicable. I/C = insufficient cases.

Source: ERS analysis of annual averages from 2006 Current Population Survey Earnings File data.

MIGRATION PATTERNS

Hired farmworkers further differentiate themselves from most other wage and salary workers because they include large numbers of mobile or migrant workers. The NAWS data set includes information on migration patterns of hired crop farmworkers, and it distinguishes between six different migrant types based on settlement, international orientation, and number of work locations (figure 15).

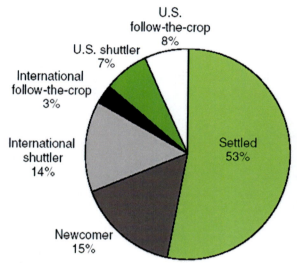

Notes: The National Agricultural Workers Survey does not survey hired livestock workers.
Source: ERS analysis of National Agricultural Workers Survey data, 1989-2006.

Figure 15. Hired crop farmworkers by migrant type, 1989-2006 averages.

Settled workers, the largest group of hired crop farmworkers, represent nonmigratory hired farmworkers. Shuttler migrants migrate between their homes and a single location. To qualify as shuttler migrants, they must travel at least 75 miles to reach their location and must work only within a 75-mile radius of that location. NAWS further distinguishes between shuttler migrants within the United States and international shuttler migrants who have crossed an international border within 12 months since they were surveyed. Thus, workers who have homes near Philadelphia but travel to Lancaster County in central Pennsylvania for 3 months to harvest vegetables are classified as U.S. shuttler migrants.

Although follow-the-crop migrants embody the popular conception of hired farmworkers, they actually comprise less than 12 percent of this workforce. Follow-the-crop workers travel to multiple U.S. farm locations for work, frequently migrating in consistent geographic patterns according to agricultural season requirements. Like shuttler migrants, follow-the-crop migrants travel more than 75 miles to a work location, but unlike shuttler migrants, they travel to *multiple* U.S. farm locations. NAWS also distinguishes between U.S. and international follow-the-crop migrants. Finally, newcomers, which NAWS classifies as international migrants, are foreign-born farmworkers residing in the United States less than 1 year and whose shuttler or follow-the-crop migration patterns remain undetermined at the time of the NAWS survey.

After 1989, the proportion of migrant crop farmworkers increased following the passage of IRCA and then declined in the late 1990s (figure 16). IRCA effectively legalized large numbers of hired farmworkers, who consequently gained sectoral and geographic mobility to seek better paying jobs. Yet, increasing use of year-round production techniques and greater border enforcement starting in the mid-1990s have reduced the proportion of migrating farmworkers.

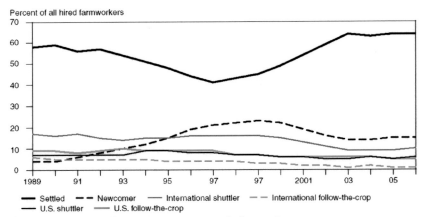

Note: Values are averaged over 3 years to smooth fluctuations.
Source: ERS analysis of National Agricultural Workers Survey data, 1989-2006.

Figure 16. Hired crop farmworkers by migrant type, trends, and 3-year moving average, 1989-2006.

Migrating hired farmworkers exhibit different demographic and employment profiles from settled farmworkers: they are younger, more likely to be male, and more often Hispanic (table 7). Disadvantages in the U.S. labor market include fewer years of education, less U.S. experience, less knowledge of English, and greater likelihood of being unauthorized (66 percent versus 27 percent). In addition, migrant farmworkers are twice as likely to work for labor contractors, who, in turn, must be reimbursed (Taylor and Thilmany, 1993; Rothenberg, 1998; Martin, 2003). Migrant farmworkers consequently earn less than settled farmworkers. In 2006, the most recent year for which NAWS data are available, average hourly wages for migrant and nonmigrant crop farmworkers were $7.52 and $8.53, respectively, a 13-percent difference.[4] Low wages of migrant farmworkers are compounded by an annual work schedule that includes half as many workweeks as for settled farmworkers.

Farmworker poverty, like low wages, has been documented extensively. According to the U.S. Bureau of Labor Statistics (BLS, 2006), the poverty rate for farming, fishing, and forestry exceeds that of all other general occupation categories (figure 17). This is the case for both men and women, as well as across four racial and ethnic categories (White, Black, Asian, and Hispanic, not shown).

Table 7. Select demographic, employment, and health characteristics of hired crop farmworkers, by migrant status, 1989-2006 averages

	Migrants	Nonmigrants
Demographic characteristics		
Median age	27	32
Percent female	14.0	29.3
Percent married	52.3	57.1
Percent Hispanic	95.3	68.1
Number children 17 and younger doing farmwork	0.57	0.17
Employment characteristics		
Median years of education	6	9
Median years of U.S. experience	3	8
Percent with no knowledge of English	66.9	33.1
Percent unauthorized	66.2	27.1
Percent employed by labor contractors	25.9	14.2
Mean wage	$6.05	$6.55
Median wage	$5.55	$6.00
Median number of weeks worked previous year	19.6	38.9
Health characteristics		
Percent with health insurance	9.1	35.3
Percent who have used health services in past 2 years	29.1	60.9
Percent reporting health condition in past 2 years	9.7	19.8

Source: ERS analysis of National Agricultural Workers Survey data, 1989-2006.

---

[4] Note that wages for 2006 differ from those recorded in table 7 which represents data from 1989 to 2006. Note also that NAWS data represent only hired crop farmworkers, and not crop and livestock farmworkers, as does the CPS.

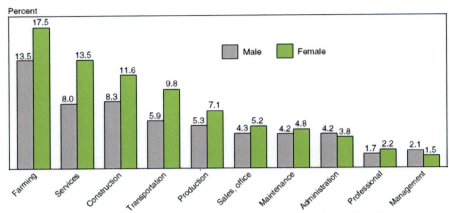

Source: "A Profile of the Working Poor," U.S. Bureau of Labor Statistics (2006).

Figure 17. Poverty rates by general occupational category, by sex, 2004.

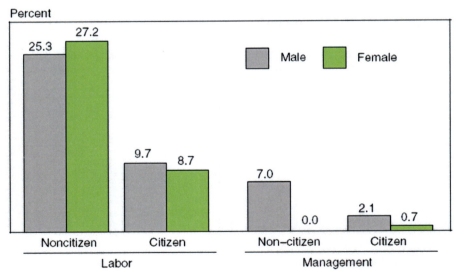

Note: Current Population Survey data are aggregated to increase statistical reliability.
Source: ERS analysis of 2005, 2006, and 2007 Current Population Survey March Supplement data.

Figure 18. Poverty status for hired farmworkers, by citizenship status, occupation category, and sex, 2006.

Morever, when this poverty rate is disaggregated by occupation category and citizenship status, the rate for noncitizen hired farm laborers jumps to 25.3 percent and 27.2 percent for men and women, respectively, compared with 9.7 percent and 8.7 percent for citizen male and female farm laborers (figure 18).

Disadvantages from migrant status extend beyond monetary compensation to health vulnerability. Less than a tenth of migrant farmworkers have health insurance, which partly explains low health service utilization rates compared with settled migrants. Another reason for lower rates may be that fewer migrant farmworkers report health problems—about half the percentage of settled migrants—owing to their relative youth and fewer years of farm labor experience.

Children of migrant workers also face numerous challenges. In addition to growing up in households with higher rates of poverty and substandard housing, they are also much more likely than the average child to move from their home schools to new schools with different curricula, testing requirements, and credit accrual rates (Baca, 2004). Migrant children must constantly adjust to new environments, and American schools do not use a viable national system for transferring records (Government Accountability Office (GAO), 1998). Despite over 30 years of concerted investment by the U.S. Department of Education's Office of Migrant Education, which facilitates educational attainment for this target population, rural migrant students continue to confront some of the most daunting learning challenges of any student population in the Nation (Salinas and Franquíz, 2004).

HOUSING CONDITIONS

Many studies have documented substandard housing conditions for hired farmworkers (McWilliams, 1935; GAO, 1971; GAO, 1989; Griffith and Kissam, 1995; Rothenberg, 1998; Martin, 2003). Farmworkers earn relatively little and either cannot afford or choose not to purchase more expensive temporary housing, relying on what is provided for them by farm operators and Federal and State government agencies. They often confront substandard housing quality, crowding, deficient sanitation, proximity to pesticides (which is especially harmful for children), and lack of inspection and enforcement (GAO, 2000; National Center for Farmworker Health, 2001; Housing Assistance Council, 2001; Quandt et al., 2004; USDA, 2004; Early et al., 2006; Lu et al., 2006; Bradman et al., 2007; Gentry et al., 2007).

CPS data indicate that housing for hired farmworkers differs from that of all workers as a group (table 8). Because hired farmworkers earn less, work shorter periods, and move frequently, they are more likely to live in crowded conditions, less likely to own their own homes, more likely to receive free housing, and more likely to live in mobile homes. Differences in housing tenure by citizenship status are particularly striking.

Farmworker housing studies that capture unauthorized workers more accurately portray more substantial differences (National Center for Farmworker Health, 2001). For example, data from a national survey of 4,600 housing units by the Housing Assistance Council (2001), a nonprofit housing research and advocacy organization, records aspects of housing conditions that affect hired farmworkers, but are not captured by other datasets, such as residential exposure to pesticides (table 9).

Table 8. Select household and housing characteristics for hired farmworkers and all U.S. households, 2005-2007

	Hired farmworkers			All U.S. households		
	Noncitizen	Citizen	Total	Noncitizen	Citizen	Total
	Number					
Household composition						
Average people in household	4.7	3.4	3.9	3.9	3.0	3.1
Average families in household	1.8	1.2	1.4	1.5	1.2	1.2
	Percent					
Housing tenure						
Own housing	24.0	69.2	52.6	40.7	74.3	71.2
Rent housing	61.8	17.6	33.9	57.1	23.6	26.8
Rent housing – no	12.7	12.5	12.6	0.8	0.9	0.9
Public housing	1.4	0.7	0.9	1.4	1.1	1.1
Housing type						
House or apartment	80.6	88.7	85.7	96.6	95.6	95.7
Mobile home, trailer, other	19.4	11.3	14.3	3.4	4.4	4.3

Note: Current Population Survey data are aggregated to increase statistical reliability.
Source: ERS analysis of 2005, 2006, and 2007 Current Population Survey March Supplement data.

Table 9. Select statistics on housing conditions

Characteristic of housing unit	Migrants	Nonmigrants
	Percent	
Overcrowded	52	3
Lacks stove	10	1
Directly adjacent to pesticide application	26	N/A

Note: N/A—not available.
Source: Housing Assistance Council 2001.

Because of lower earnings and a greater likelihood of remitting earnings to family members in their countries of origin, unauthorized workers are more likely to conserve earnings by living in overcrowded housing. Housing Assistance Council data suggest that half of all hired crop farmworkers live in overcrowded conditions[5] compared with 3 percent of all wage and salary workers. The data also indicate that the prevalence and degree (number of people sharing a room) of overcrowding vary according to legal status, with unauthorized workers experiencing higher rates than authorized and citizen workers (data not shown).

A limited housing supply hinders those wishing to purchase homes, particularly in rural agricultural areas and where large groups of farmworkers have settled with their families to become year-round residents. Migrant workers may be unable to meet credit checks, provide requested deposits, or engage in extended contracts. Landlords may be reluctant to rent to hired farm-workers out of fear that they may overcrowd rental units as an economic strategy. In some cases, housing may be in such short supply that hired farmworkers must remain homeless for extended periods, obtaining shelter wherever they can—including in fields, in cars, or under bridges (GAO, 1989; USDA, 2004).

Migrant housing is regulated under the Migrant and Seasonal Agricultural Worker Protection Act (MSPA), whose rules are enforced by the Wage and Hour Division of the U.S. Department of Labor's (DOL) Employment Standards Administration. States also have their own housing laws, and farm operators must abide by the more stringent of the laws. Farm operators are not required to provide farmworker housing, but if they do, they are required to ensure that their housing complies with substantive Federal and State safety and health standards. Yet, according to these same regulations, such protections apply only to

---

[5] NAWS data on hired crop farmworkers from 1989 to 2006 indicate this figure stands at 85 percent.

farmworkers hired directly by farm operators, not to individuals hired through labor contractors.

From the farm operator perspective, migrant housing represents a considerable capital investment to meet temporary housing demands during labor-intensive processes such as planting or harvesting. Farmers are more likely to make such investments for year-round workers. In one government survey, growers cited the H2-A visa program's housing provision requirement for their lack of program participation (GAO, 1989). Farmworker housing, therefore, remains a contentious issue, encompassing ongoing challenges for both farm operators—who may invest in it and are required to meet Federal and State farmworker housing guidelines if they do—and farmworkers and their advocates, who contend that much of it is substandard.

USDA administers a well-established Federal program known as the Section 514/5 16 Farm Labor Housing Program which provides funding to buy, build, improve, or repair housing for farm laborers (USDA, 2004; Housing Assistance Council, 2006). In addition, some States with the largest populations of hired farmworkers, such as Florida and California, have created model programs and led efforts to provide affordable housing and workable housing code enforcement (National Center for Farmworker Health, 2001). Assessments of farmworker housing in agricultural areas offer thorough descriptions of local conditions and policy recommendations for improvements (Housing Assistance Council, 1997; Washington State Housing Finance Commission (WSHFC), 2006; Strochlic et al., 2007).

HEALTH

Agriculture is among the more hazardous industries in the United States, and farmworker health remains a considerable occupational concern for this sector (National Institute for Occupational Safety and Health (NIOSH), 1992; Pratt and Hard, 1998; Loh and Richardson, 2004). While farmworkers face workplace hazards similar to those found in other industrial settings, such as working with heavy machinery and hard physical labor, they also confront factors more common to agricultural production such as pesticide exposure, sun exposure, inadequate sanitary facilities, and crowded and/or substandard housing. Young farmworkers face greater risks of agricultural industry accidents because of their lack of experience.

A number of Federal and State programs serving the general public and/or farmworkers provide medical care as well as financial support for disabled workers. These include Medicaid, Social Security, State farmworker housing programs, and the Migrant Health Program. Yet, inadequate enforcement of Federal regulations and lack of program participation put farmworkers, particularly migrant farmworkers, at greater health risk (Sakala, 1987; GAO, 1992; Reeves and Schafer, 2003; Shipp et al., 2005). Apart from government programs, hired farmworkers typically cannot afford quality health care and often work in locations with limited access to medical facilities.

Two key indicators measuring occupational health risk include fatalities and the incidence of injuries and illnesses.[6] Data from the 1996 and 2006 Department of Labor's Census of Fatal Occupational Injuries indicate that in many industrial sectors, fatalities have declined following general improvements in occupational safety. The data, however, do not indicate the same degree of improvement for the agricultural sector, where fatality rates have increased (figure 19).[7] This outcome is consistent with other government research on fatalities among foreign-born workers, whose increasing incidence of occupational fatalities exceeds their increasing proportion in the U.S. labor force (Dong and Platner, 2004; Loh and Richardson, 2004; Richardson et al., 2004). As a result, between 1996 and 2001, the agriculture, forestry, and fishing sector, which employed less than 2 percent of the U.S. workforce, accounted for a disproportionate 13 percent of all fatal occupational injuries (Loh and Richardson, 2004).

The agricultural sector also exhibits some of the highest rates of occupational injuries and illnesses of all industrial sectors (figure 20). These incidents have declined consistently over time, following similar patterns in other industrial sectors.

---

[6] In order to present incident and fatality rate data across the most recent 10-year period, this section focuses on statistics by industry rather than by occupation. Within the agriculture industry sector, fatality rates vary substantially by subsector. In 2006, both forestry (85.6), and fishing and hunting (95.9) displayed significantly higher fatality rates than crop production (33.0), animal production (16.2), or support activities (26.3). The two former subsectors, however, account for less than 10 percent of all employment within the agricultural sector. Moreover, within the agricultural sector are numerous occupations for which fatality and injury rates can differ considerably. Forestry, fishing, and hunting occupations have much higher rates that reflect industry differences noted above. In addition, ranchers, farmers, and managers have a combined rate (29.6) that is notably higher than that of miscellaneous farm- workers (21.7).

[7] While changes between 2 selected years may reflect random fluctuation, the trend between these points across all 10 years does not reflect a clear trend downward or upward. Note that between 2002 and 2003, the BLS revised its industrial classifications from the SIC to the NAICS typology. Such a change does not significantly hamper comparisons across time at the level of industrial sector aggregation presented. The two agricultural subsectors of crop and livestock agriculture presented were not affected by the change in classification systems.

Data from NAWS illustrate the pervasiveness of some physical ailments (table 10), although comparisons are complicated by the lack of data for the U.S. employed population. Some rates, such as 8 percent of respondents reporting skin problems or 20 percent reporting musculoskeletal problems within the past year, are above national averages (Villarejo and Baron, 1999). Twelve percent of all farmworkers responding to the survey indicated they had worked with pesticides in the previous 12 months. Even relatively low levels of incidents, such as treatment for pesticide exposure, have considerable implications for long-term health (GAO, 1992). About 3 percent of those using pesticides were under age 18, making the consequences of such occupational hazards longer lasting over the course of these workers' lives (GAO, 2000).

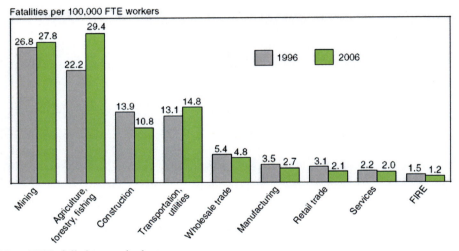

Note: FTE=full-time equivalent.
Source: Bureau of Labor Statistics, U.S. Department of Labor, Survey of Occupational Injuries, 1996-2006.

Figure 19. Fatality rates, by industrial sector, 1996 and 2006.

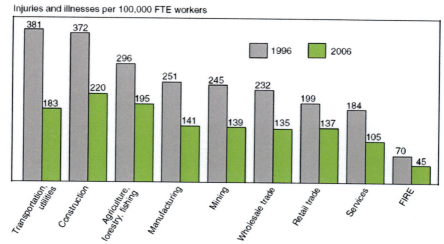

Note: FTE=full-time equivalent. Estimates for the agricultural sector exclude farms with fewer than 11 employees and include injuries for farm operators as well as all farm labor.

Source: Bureau of Labor Statistics, U.S. Department of Labor, Survey of Occupational Injuries and Illnesses in cooperation with participating State agencies.

Figure 20. Incidences of injuries and illnesses involving days away from work, by industrial sector, 1996 and 2006.

The absence of adequate plumbing facilities at agricultural worksites poses health hazards for workers who constantly work in soiled conditions, particularly those who work with pesticides (figure 21). Lack of drinking water poses a significant health threat to farmworkers who face hazards of dehydration and heat stroke. When NAWS data were first collected, 15 percent of all workers cited a lack of toilets and 20 percent a lack of washing water. Those rates have declined significantly in subsequent years. While 1 in 4 workers complained about the lack of at least one of the three sanitary facilities noted in 1989, the figure had fallen to 1 in 10 by 2006. NAWS data also indicate that workers lacking legal status are about 50 percent more likely to lack access to a sanitary facility than workers with legal status (data not shown).

NAWS data also report what crop farmworkers cited as obstacles to their obtaining health care (table 11). Two-thirds of all farmworkers cited costs, and almost a third cited language barriers to explain their inability to obtain health care when needed. Within the hired crop farmworker population, unauthorized workers were almost twice as likely as authorized workers and three times as likely as citizen workers to report such obstacles.

Table 10. Select health indicators for hired crop farmworkers

	Unauthorized	Authorized	Citizen	All
	Percent			
Physical ailments[1]				
Had any work-related injury or accident in past 12 months	1.4	2.3	2.2	1.8
Experienced wheezing or whistling in chest at any time	4.9	5.9	6.1	5.4
Had any skin problem in past 12 months	7.9	7.7	9.0	8.1
Had any musculoskeletal problem in past 12 months	17.8	21.6	21.9	19.7
Pesticide application[2]				
Used (loaded, mixed, or applied pesticides) in past 12 months	5.9	12.6	5.9	12.3
Under age 21; used pesticides in past 12 months	7.6	0.3	6.2	5.5
Under age 18; used pesticides in past 12 months	I/C	I/C	I/C	2.8
Treated for pesticide exposure in past 12 months (1999-2003)	0.9	0.6	1.3	0.9
Pesticide training[3]				
Received training in safe use of pesticides in last 12 months (2002-2006)	65.1	77.2	71.1	69.4
Used pesticides in past 12 months and received training during same period	87.8	92.7	95.8	93.1

[1] 1999-2004.
[2] 1999-2006.
[3] 1994-2004 except last question, 2002-2006.
Note: I/C— insufficient cases.
Source: National Agricultural Workers Survey, 1989-2006.

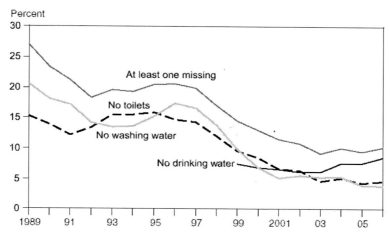

Note: Values are averaged over 3 years to smooth fluctuations. Questions on drinking water availability did not appear on National Agricultural Workers Survey until 1999.
Source: ERS analysis of National Agriculutral Workers Survey data, 1989-2006.

Figure 21. Unsanitary conditions for hired crop farmworkers, 1989-2006 Percent.

NAWS data indicate that almost three-quarters of crop farmworkers possess some type of health insurance in case of injury, and almost half receive some compensation from their employer while recuperating if injuries prevent them from working (table 12). Few workers receive health insurance for nonwork-related injuries or illnesses. Access to programs varies according to legal status, a reflection of U.S. experience and the ability to obtain employment with firms that offer such benefits (table 13).

Health insurance benefits provided in case of an injury should be distinguished from general health insurance. Only a fourth of crop farmworkers surveyed by NAWS between 2000 and 2006 stated that they had general health insurance. Farmworkers estimated the health insurance coverage of their spouses at roughly the same proportion, and farmworkers' children, who are often eligible for government support, were twice as likely to have health insurance.

Other farmworker health concerns not addressed in this report include dental health, tuberculosis, and mental illness (Arcury and Quandt, 1998; Villarejo, 2003). Health practitioners also cite HIV/AIDS as a growing concern among the farmworker population that may have repercussions in countries of origin (Sanchez et al., 2004). Several studies indicate that farmworkers are less likely than other wage and salary employees to receive financial or disability support from the Social

Security program when they retire or become disabled (GAO, 1992; Lacar, 2001).

Table 11. Reasons given by hired crop farmworkers for inaccessible health care

	Unauthorized	Authorized	Citizen	All
			Percent	
Too expensive	59	73	68	64
Don't speak my language	38	20	3	29
Other	22	23	26	23
Don't know where services located	14	3	4	10
I'm unauthorized and they don't treat me well	12	1	0	7
Transportation	8	4	6	7
Don't feel welcome	5	6	3	5
Don't understand my problems	4	4	2	4
Don't have services needed	2	2	5	2
Will lose my job	2	2	1	2
Health center not open when needed	2	1	2	2
Percent experiencing obstacles to health care access	42	24	14	29

Notes: The question on obstacles to health care access was not asked prior to 1993. Columns do not equal 100 percent because respondents could check off more than one reason. Source: National Agricultural Workers Survey, 1993-2006.

Table 12. Employer financial support for injured farmworkers, by legal status

	Unauthorized	Authorized	Citizen	All
	Percent			
Health insurance if injured on the job and sick from work	67.0	76.7	78.7	73.5
Workers' compensation if injured on the job and sick from work	36.8	46.9	59.7	47.2
Health insurance if injured off the job and sick from work	4.5	11.8	16.0	9.5

Source: National Agricultural Workers Survey, 1989-2006.

Table 13. Health insurance coverage of farmworkers and their family members, by legal status

	Unauthorized	Authorized	Citizen	All
	Percent			
Farmworker has health insurance	9.8	29.4	51.7	24.5
Spouse has health insurance	11.0	31.5	58.0	28.7
Children have health insurance	36.4	58.3	76.3	52.7

Note: This particular health insurance question was not asked prior to 2000. Source: National Agricultural Workers Survey, 2000-2006.

USE OF SOCIAL SERVICES

Given their health hazards and substantially lower wages, hired farmworkers would be expected to utilize public services at higher rates than nonagricultural wage and salary workers. However, roughly half of all crop farmworkers and an undetermined yet substantial proportion of livestock farmworkers lack legal authorization, which limits their access to certain Federal public services. States may have eligibility requirements for their programs that permit unauthorized resident participation or that differ significantly from those of Federal programs. In all cases, previous research shows that unauthorized U.S. residents utilize public services less than authorized residents or citizens because of concerns about possible deportation (Chavez, 1997; Berk and Schur, 2001; Kullgren, 2003).

Yet, according to CPS data, which capture only a small portion of the unauthorized population, utilization is more prevalent among hired farmworkers and their households than for all wage and salary workers (table 14). In addition, utilization is more prevalent among noncitizens than citizens for both groups of workers. Farmworker households, on average, have 50 percent more children under age 15, and those children are twice as likely to receive Medicaid and qualify for free/reduced-price school lunch. One benefit of the School Lunch Program is that farmworkers' children apparently enjoy the benefits of regular hot school meals at least as much as children of other wage and salary workers. Farmworker households do not appear to benefit more than the broader employed population from housing assistance programs and Medicare. They are far more likely to receive food stamps, WIC, and Medicaid owing, in part, to eligibility of citizen children for these programs. Receipt of unemployment, workers', and disability compensation is roughly 50 percent higher for hired farmworkers than for wage and salary employees in general.

One cannot make inferences about the utilization rates of unauthorized workers from CPS data because the noncitizen category includes authorized and unauthorized workers. NAWS data, however, provide evidence of clear differences in public service utilization by legal status (figure 22). According to these data, which capture unauthorized, authorized, and citizen legal statuses, authorized crop farmworkers show above-average participation in five social welfare programs captured in the NAWS data compared with unauthorized workers who show below-average participation. Citizen farmworkers, whose poverty rates are a third of noncitizen farmworkers, utilize these programs less than authorized workers.

Table 14. Use of social services by child, household, employment, and household structure category, 2005-2007

	Hired farmworkers			All U.S. households		
	Noncitiz	Citizen	Total	Noncitizen	Citizen	Total
	Percent					
Children Children in household covered by Medicaid	27.9	10.3	16.6	16.0	6.2	7.1
Children who qualify for free/reduced lunch	79.1	36.5	53.1	55.1	22.1	25.9
Children who usually eat a hot lunch	78.3	75.2	76.4	71.5	65.4	66.1
Households						
Renters living in public housing	2.0	2.3	2.1	2.4	4.2	3.9
Renters receiving govt. housing assistance	0.5	0.7	0.6	1.3	2.1	1.9
Anyone in household receives food stamps	10.2	4.5	6.5	4.6	3.4	3.5
Anyone in household receives WIC	21.2	7.6	14.2	10.4	7.0	7.4
Anyone in household covered by Medicare	4.3	13.1	10.0	6.0	9.8	9.4
Anyone in household covered by Medicaid	40.6	20.8	27.8	24.8	11.9	13.0
Employment						
Anyone in household receives unempl. comp.	8.4	9.0	8.8	3.9	5.9	5.7
Anyone in household receives workers' comp.	2.4	2.2	2.3	1.3	1.4	1.4

	Hired farmworkers			All U.S. households		
	Noncitiz	Citizen	Total	Noncitizen	Citizen	Total
	Percent					
Anyone in household receives dis. benefits	1.6	1.3	1.4	0.7	1.0	1.0
	Number					
Household structure						
Average number under age 15 per household	1.40	0.71	0.96	0.99	0.65	0.68
Average number of families in household	1.71	1.16	1.35	1.46	1.20	1.22

Note: Current Population Survey data are aggregated to increase statistical reliability.
Source: ERS analysis of 2005, 2006, and 2007 Current Population Survey March Supplement data.

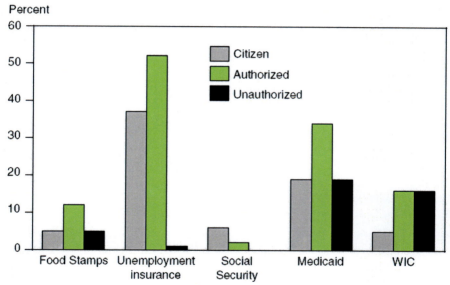

Notes: Social service utilization by farmworkers occurs within the 2 years before the interview. Unauthorized immigrants are eligible for WIC and citizen children of unauthorized immigrants are eligible for Food Stamps and Medicaid.
Source: ERS analysis of combined National Agricultural Workers Survey data, 2004-2006.

Figure 22. Social service utilization of crop farmworkers, by legal status, 2004-2006.

FINDINGS AND IMPLICATIONS

In the past several decades, the U.S. economy has undergone enormous changes, including broad-based industrial restructuring, service sector growth, technological innovation, and expanding globalization. Within the agricultural sector, technological change has increased productivity while reducing the use of farm labor. Future demand for hired farm labor depends on the relative weights of several opposing trends:

- Increased mechanization, technological advances, and growing acceptance and consumption of imported food, reducing the demand for hired farm labor; and
- Increased farm consolidation and greater consumer demand for year-round fresh fruits, vegetables, and more labor-intensive organic produce, maintaining or increasing the demand for hired farmworkers.

Contrasting these dynamic trends are the conditions and circumstances for hired agricultural workers who, as a group, remain among the most disadvantaged employees in the United States. Compared with workers in other sectors of the economy, a substantial proportion of farmworkers are foreign born and lack legal status, English language facility, and U.S. working or living experience. They are also younger and possess less education than most U.S. workers.

Agricultural work often serves as an entry point into the U.S. labor market and one from which significant numbers of workers exit when other more remunerative, less arduous, and more stable employment becomes available. Compared with many other wage and salary workers, hired farmworkers face more physically grueling and hazardous working conditions and substandard living conditions. Despite improvements in policy and labor enforcement, numerous studies demonstrate that farmworkers continue to be subjected to a range of unfair labor practices (Commission on Security and Cooperation in Europe, 1993; Edid, 1994; Griffith and Kissam, 1995; Rothenberg, 1998; Ruckelshaus and Goldstein, 2002; Martin, 2003; Southern Poverty Law Center, 2007). Hired farmworkers use social services at higher rates than other wage and salary workers, as a group, although access is limited by the unauthorized legal status of many.

Demands for changes to current immigration policies in the wake of a rapidly growing and geographically diverse foreign-born population, the events of 9/11, and discussions surrounding agricultural legislation such as the 2008 Farm Bill have increased the visibility of the hired-farm labor population among policymakers and the general public.

As of early 2008, several proposed immigration law reforms had been offered, notably AgJobs which is directly related to agricultural workers. Representing a compromise between growers, farm labor advocates, and Federal legislators, the AgJobs legislation would provide farmworkers with temporary citizenship status and the possibility of obtaining permanent legal residence in the United States.

AgJobs would also restructure the existing H-2A visa program to reduce administrative burdens for growers, while increasing legal protections for workers. The H-2A visa program, which in 2005 involved 64,000 workers out of an estimated 2.5 million engaged in hired farmwork (less than 2 percent), remains the only legally sanctioned guestworker program. According to both growers and worker advocates, however, the program remains flawed. Growers object to what they consider cumbersome administrative requirements, while farmworker advocates contend that the program invites pervasive abuses through a lack of regulatory enforcement. To address border security and immigration challenges, President Bush recently issued a directive to the Department of Labor to review H-2A program regulations and institute changes that tackle concerns of both growers and farm labor advocates.

Current legislative and public debates on immigration reform underscore the importance of unauthorized workers to certain sectors of the U.S. economy, particularly agriculture. Several studies based on the experience with IRCA estimate that if unauthorized workers were granted legal status, their agricultural wages would increase significantly, and they may be less likely to take seasonal agricultural production jobs (Taylor, 1992; Koussoudji and Cobb-Clark, 2000). Hence, those employing seasonal workers would face the greatest financial challenges resulting from labor market constriction due to immigration reform (American Farm Bureau Federation, 2006). Owner- operators are likely to adjust over time by acquiring additional capital equipment, switching commodities, or possibly ceasing agricultural production.

Hired crop farmworkers, on the other hand, display consistency regarding their expectations for future farmwork (figure 23). NAWS data suggest that over 80 percent of all workers expect to continue doing farmwork for 4 or more years from the time they were surveyed. Except for a decline during 1995-2000, these expectations have remained stable over the entire 17-year NAWS data collection span. This suggests that, while a portion of hired farmworkers cycle through agricultural employment, using farm labor as a stepping stone to other opportunities within the U.S. labor market, most expect to remain in the agricultural sector for the foreseeable future.

Implications for change in farm labor and immigration policy extend beyond U.S. borders. An estimated 8 of every 10 hired farmworkers are foreign-born. Many have families in their countries of origin that they support through remitted earnings. Consequently, changing employment conditions for farm-workers in the United States can have economic consequences for communities in other countries.

One important finding relates to the shift from seasonal to year-round agricultural employment. Results show that migrant hired farmworkers work half as many weeks per year as nonmigrant hired farmworkers. Current research and industry trends indicate a growing tendency to switch from seasonal to year-round workers, corresponding in part to growing year-round domestic demand for fresh fruits and vegetables. In turn, migrant workers are settling permanently in places where they previously worked temporarily (DOL, 2005).

As seasonal workers transition into year-round workers by performing other tasks, both farm operators and hired farmworkers benefit—the former from a more stable and available workforce and the latter from improved economic conditions. The Department of Labor reports a correlation between the number of years worked for a single employer and the likelihood of working year round. Year-round workers also report higher rates of pay and greater benefits (DOL, 2005).

While this report attempts to provide a reasonably broad overview of the hired-farmworker population, an exhaustive survey of all issues related to this population is beyond its scope (Goldstein et al., 2006). Topics not mentioned include farmworker mental health; food security of farmworker families; nutrition, given the pervasiveness of fast food diets among farm-workers (Poss and Pierce, 2003; Cason et al., 2003; Weigel, 2007); substance abuse, gangs, and sexually transmitted diseases in migrant farmworker communities; farmworker youth education and health outcomes; and State variation in workers' compensation coverage.

Six States – California, Florida, Washington, Texas, Oregon, and North Carolina – account for half of the Nation's expenditure on hired labor. Any innovative or "best practices" and regulations that these States develop regarding hired farmworkers may provide lessons and set standards and innovations for the rest of the country.

REFERENCES

Allen, Richard, and Virginia Harris. *What We Know About the Demographics of U.S. Farm Operators, paper presented at the 2005 Agricultural Outlook*

Conference, Crystal City, VA. Available at http://www.agcensus.usda.gov/Publications/2002/Other_Analysis/demographicpaper022505.pdf.

American Farm Bureau Federation. *Impact of Migrant Labor Restrictions on the Agricultural Sector*, 2006.

Arcury, T., and S. Quandt. "Occupational and Environmental Health Risks in Farm Labor," *Human Organization* 57(3): 331–4, 1998.

Baca, Leonard. "Foreword," *Scholars in the Fields: The Challenges of Migrant Education*, Cynthia Salinas and María E. Franquíz (eds.), Charleston, WV: Education Resources Information Center (ERIC), Clearinghouse on Rural Education and Small Schools, 2004.

Berk, Marc L., and Claudia L. Schur. "The Effect of Fear on Access to Care Among Undocumented Latino Immigrants," *Journal of Immigrant Health* 3(3): 1096-4045, 2001.

Bradman A., D. Whitaker, L. Quiros, R. Castorina, B.C. Henn, N. Nishioka, J. Morgan, D.B. Barr, M.E. Harnly, J.A. Brisbin, L.S. Sheldon, T.E. McKone, and B. Eskanazi. "Pesticides and their Metabolites in the Homes and Urine of Farmworker Children Living in the Salinas Valley, CA," *Journal of Exposure Science and Environmental Epidemiology*, 17(4):331-49, 2007.

Cason, K.L., S. Nieto-Montenegro, A. Chavez-Martinez, N. Lee, and A. Snyder. "Dietary Intake and Food Security Among Migrant Farmworkers in Pennsylvania," unpublished technical report, joint ERS Food and Nutrition Research Small Grants Program, 2003.

Chavez, Leo. *Shadowed Lives: Undocumented Immigrants in American Society*, New York: Harcourt Brace, 1997.

Commission on Security and Cooperation in Europe. *Migrant Farmworkers in the United States, Implementation of the Helsinki Accords, Briefings*, U.S. Government Printing Office, 1993.

Dimitri, Carolyn, Anne Effland, and Neilson Conklin. *The 20th Century Transformation of U.S. Agriculture and Farm Policy*, Economic Information Bulletin No. 3, U.S. Department of Agriculture, Economic Research Service, 2005.

Dong, X., and J.W. Platner. "Occupational Fatalities of Hispanic Construction Workers From 1992 to 2000," *American Journal of Industrial Medicine* 45:45–54, 2004.

Early J., S.W. Davis, S.A. Quandt, P. Rao, B.M. Snively, and T.A. Arcury. "Housing Characteristics of Farmworker Families in North Carolina," *Journal of Immigrant and Minority Health*, 8(2): 173-84, 2006.

Edid, Maralyn. *Farm Labor Organizing: Trends and Prospects*, Ithaca, NY: ILR Press, 1994.

Fuglie, Keith O., James M. MacDonald, and Eldon Ball. *Productivity Growth in U.S. Agriculture*, Economic Brief No. 9, U.S. Department of Agriculture, Economic Research Service, 2007.

Gentry, A.L., J.G. Grzywacz, S.A. Quandt, Davis, S.W., and, T.A. Arcury. "Housing Quality Among North Carolina Farmworker Families, *Journal of Agricultural Safety and Health*, 13(3):323-37, 2007.

Goldstein, Bruce, Ed Kissam, Mark Miller, and Rick Mines. *Proposed National Farmworker Research Agenda: Topics, Methodologies, and Institutional Framework*, Oakland, CA: Aguirre International and The Farmworker Justice Fund, 2006.

Government Accountability Office (GAO). *Impact of Federal Programs to Improve the Living Conditions of Migrant and Other Seasonal Farmworkers*, Report No. B177486, 1971.

_____. *Immigration Reform: Potential Impact on West Coast Farm Labor*, Report HRD 89/89, 1989.

_____. *Hired Farmworkers: Health and Well-being at Risk*, Report HRD-92-46, 1992.

_____. *H2-A Agricultural Guestworker Program: Changes Could Improve Services to Employers and Better Protect Workers*, Health and Human Services Division Report No. 98-20, 1997.

_____. *Child Labor in Agriculture: Changes Needed to Better Protect Health and Educational Opportunities*, Report GAO/HEHS-98-193, 1998.

_____. *Pesticides: Improvements Needed to Ensure the Safety of Farmworkers and Their Children*, Report GAO/RCED-00-40, 2000.

_____. *Child Labor: Labor Can Strengthen Its Efforts to Protect Children Who Work*, Report GAO-02-880, 2002.

_____. *Decennial Census: Lessons Learned for Locating and Counting Migrant and Seasonal Farm Workers*, Report GAO-03-605, 2003.

Griffith, David. *American Guestworkers: Jamaicans and Mexicans in the U.S. Labor Market*, University Park, PA: Penn State University Press, 2006.

Griffith, David, and Ed Kissam. *Working Poor: Farmworkers in the United States*, Philadelphia, PA: Temple University Press, 1995.

Hoppe, Robert A., and Penni Korb. "Large and Small Farms: Trends and Characteristics," *Structural and Financial Characteristics of U.S. Farms: 2004 Family Farm Report*, David E. Banker and James M. MacDonald (eds.), AIB-797, U.S. Department of Agriculture, Economic Research Service, 2005.

Housing Assistance Council. *Housing for Families and Unaccompanied Migrant Farmworkers*, 1997.

_____. *No Refuge from the Fields: Findings from a Survey of Farmworker Housing Conditions in the United States*, 2001.

_____. *USDA Section 514/516 Farmworker Housing: Existing Stock and Changing Needs*, 2006.

Isé, S., and J. Perloff. "Legal Status and Earnings of Agricultural Workers," *American Journal of Agricultural Economics*, 77:375-86, 1995.

Kandel, William, and John Cromartie. *New Patterns of Hispanic Settlement in Rural America*, RDRR-99, U.S. Department of Agriculture, Economic Research Service, 2004.

Khan, M. Akhtar, Philip Martin, and Phil Hardiman. *California's Farm Labor Markets: A Cross-Sectional Analysis of Employment and Earnings in 1991, 1996, and 2001*, Sacramento, CA: Applied Research Unit, Labor Market Information Division, California Employment Development Department, 2003.

Kossoudji, Sherrie A., and Deborah A. Cobb-Clark. "IRCA's Impact on the Mobility and Occupational Concentration of Newly Legalized Men," *Journal of Population Economics*, 13: 81-98, 2000.

Kullgren, Jeffrey T. "Restrictions on Undocumented Immigrants' Access to Health Services: The Public Health Implications of Welfare Reform," *American Journal of Public Health*, 93(10): 1630-33, 2003.

Lacar, Marvi S. "The Personal Responsibility and Work Opportunity Reconciliation Act of 1996: Implications for Hispanic Migrant Farmworkers," *Working Paper No. 53*, Lansing, MI: Julien Samora Research Institute, Michigan State University, 2001.

Larson, Janelle M., Jill L. Findeis, Hema Swaminathan, and Qiuyan Wang. "A Comparison of Data Sources for Hired Farm Labor Research: The NAWS and the CPS," *The Dynamics of Hired Farm Labor*, Jill L. Findeis, Ann M. Vandeman, Janelle M. Larson, and Jack L. Runyan (eds.), New York, NY: CABI Publishing, 2002.

Levine, Linda. *Farm Labor Shortages and Immigration Policy*, RL30395, Congressional Research Service, 2007.

Loh, Katherine, and Scott Richardson. "Foreign-born Workers: Trends in Fatal Occupational Injuries, 1996-2001," *Monthly Labor Review* (June): 42-53, 2004.

Lu C., R.A. Fenske, N.J. Simcox, and D. Kalman. "Pesticide Exposure of Children in an Agricultural Community: Evidence of Household Proximity to Farmland and Take Home Exposure Pathways," *Environmental Research*, 84(3):290-302, 2006.

Martin, Philip. *Promise Unfulfilled: Unions, Immigration, and the Farm Workers*, Ithaca, NY: Cornell University Press, 2003.

———. "Immigration Reform: Implications for Agriculture," *Agricultural and Resource Economics Update*, Davis, CA: University of California, Giannini Foundation, 2006.

———. "Immigration Reform, Agriculture, and Rural Communities," *Choices* 22(1): 43-47, 2007.

———. "Farm Labor Shortages: How Real? What Response?" *Backg rounder*, Washington, DC: Center for Immigration Studies, November 2007.

Martin, Philip, Michael Fix, and J. Edward Taylor. *The New Rural Poverty: Agriculture and Immigration in California*, Washington, DC: Urban Institute Press, 2006.

Massey, Douglas S., Jorge Durand, and Nolan J. Malone. *Beyond Smoke and Mirrors: Mexican Immigration in an Era of Economic Integration*, New York: Russell Sage Foundation, 2002.

McWilliams, Carey. *Factories in the Fields*, Berkeley, CA: University of California Press, 1935.

Mehta, K., S.M. Gabbard, V. Barrat, M. Lewis, D. Carroll, and R. Mines. *Findings from the National Agricultural Workers Survey (NAWS) 1 997-1998: A Demographic and Employment Profile of United States Farmworkers*, U.S. Department of Labor, 2000.

National Agricultural Statistics Service, USDA. Data downloaded on May 29, 2007 from http://www.nass.usda.gov/Charts_and_Maps/graphics/data/ fl_qtrwk.txt.

National Center for Farmworker Health. *Migrant Health Issues*, National Advisory Council on Migrant Health by the National Center For Farmworker Health, Inc., Buda, TX, 2001.

National Institute for Occupational Safety and Health (NIOSH). *Papers and Proceedings of the Surgeon General's Conference on Agricultural Safety and Health*, DHHS (NIOSH) Publication number 92-105, Cincinnati, OH: U.S. Department of Health and Human Services, Centers for Disease Control and Prevention, 1992.

———. *NIOSH Alert: Preventing Deaths, Injuries, and Illnesses of Young Workers*, Publication number 2003-128, Cincinnati, OH: U.S. Department of Health and Human Services, Centers for Disease Control and Prevention, 2003.

Oliveira, Victor J., and E.J. Cox. *The Agricultural Workforce of 1987: A Statistical Profile*, AER-609, U.S. Department of Agriculture, Economic Research Service, 1990.

Poss, J.E., and R. Pierce. "Characteristics of Selected Migrant Farmworkers in West Texas and Southern New Mexico," *Californian Journal of Health Promotion*, 1(2): 138-147, 2003.

Pratt, S.G., and D.L. Hard. "Injury Risk Factors Associated with Agricultural Workplace Fatalities," *Journal of Agricultural Safety and Health*, Special Issue (1): 29-38, 1998.

Quandt S.A., T.A. Arcury, Rao P. Snively, D.E. Camann, A.M. Doran, A.Y. Yau, J.S. Hoppin, and D.S. Jackson. "Agricultural and Residential Pesticides in Wipe Samples from Farmworker Family Residences in North Carolina and Virginia," *Environmental Health Perspectives*, 1 12(3):382-7, 2004.

Reeves, Margaret, and Kristin S. Schafer. "Greater Risks, Fewer Rights: U.S. Farmworkers and Pesticides," *International Journal of Occupational and Environmental Health,* 9(1): 30-39, 2003.

Richardson, David B., Dana Loomis, James Bena, and A. John Bailer. "Fatal Occupational Injury Rates in Southern and Non-Southern States, by Race and Hispanic Ethnicity," *American Journal of Public Health*, 94:1756-1761, 2004.

Rivera-Batiz, F. "Unauthorized Workers in the Labor Market: An Analysis of the Earnings of Legal and Illegal Mexican Immigrants in the United States," *Journal of Population Economics,* 12(1):91- 116, 1999.

Rothenberg, Daniel. *With These Hands: The Hidden World of Migrant Farmworkers Today*, Berkeley: University of California Press, 1998.

Ruckelshaus, Catherine, and Bruce Goldstein. "From Orchards to the Internet: Confronting Contingent Work Abuses," New York: National Employment Law Project, 2002.

Runyan, Jack. *Profile of Hired Farmworkers, 1998 Annual Averages*, AER-790, U.S. Department of Agriculture, Economic Research Service, 2000.

Sakala, Carol. "Migrant and Seasonal Farmworkers in the United States: A Review of Health Hazards, Status, and Policy," *International Migration Review*, 21(3): 659-687, 1987.

Salinas, Cynthia, and María E. Franquíz (eds.). *Scholars in the Field: The Challenges of Migrant Education*, Charleston, WV: ERIC Clearinghouse on Rural Education and Small Schools, 2004.

Sanchez, Melissa, George F. Lemp, Carlos Magis-Rodriguez, Enrique Bravo- Garcia, Susan Carter, and Juan D. Ruiz. "The Epidemiology of HIV Among Mexican Migrants and Recent Immigrants in California and Mexico," *Journal of Acquired Immune Deficiency Syndromes*, 37(S4):S204-S214, 2004.

Shipp, Eva M., Sharon P. Cooper, Keith D. Burau, and Jane N. Bolin. "Pesticide Safety Training and Access to Field Sanitation Among Migrant Farmworker

Mothers from Starr County, Texas," *Journal of Agricultural Safety and Health*, 11(1): 51–60, 2005.

Southern Poverty Law Center. *Close to Slavery: Guestworker Programs in the United States*, Mobile, AL, 2007.

Strochlic, Ron, Don Villarejo, Sandra Nichols, Cathy Wirth, and Raoul Liévanos. *An Assessment of the Demand for Farm Worker Housing in Napa Valley*, Davis, CA: California Institute for Rural Studies, 2007.

Taylor, J. Edward. "Earnings and Mobility of Legal and Illegal Immigrant Workers in Agriculture," *American Journal of Agricultural Economics*, 74: 889-896, 1992.

Taylor, J. Edward, and Dawn Thilmany. "Worker Turnover, Farm Labor Contractors, and IRCA's Impact on the California Farm Labor Market," *American Journal of Agricultural Economics*, 75(2): 350-360, 1993.

U.S. Department of Agriculture (USDA), Rural Development. *Building a Better Future for Farmworkers*, Report PA1669, 2004.

U.S. Department of Commerce, Census Bureau. "Technical Documentation," *Summary File 3, 2000 Census of Population and Housing*, 2002.

_____. American FactFinder: http://factfinder.census.gov/home/saff/main.html?_lang=en, accessed April 9, 2007.

U.S. Department of Health and Human Services. *National Occupational Research Agenda (NORA): Update, July 1998*, Report No. 98-134, 1998.

U.S. Department of Labor (DOL). *National Agricultural Workers Survey* 2001-2002, 2005.

_____. *H-2A Regional Summary, Fiscal Year 2006, Annual*, http://www.foreignlaborcert.doleta.gov/h-2a_region2006.cfm, accessed November 5, 2007.

U.S. Department of Labor, Bureau of Labor Statistics. *A Profile of the Working Poor, 2004*, Report 994, 2006.

_____. Bureau of Labor Statistics, Census of Fatal Occupational Injuries, 1996 and 2006.

_____. Bureau of Labor Statistics, Survey of Occupational Injuries and Illnesses, 1996 and 2006.

Villarejo, D. "The Health of U.S. Hired FarmWorkers," *Annual Review of Public Health*, 24:175–93, 2003.

Villarejo, D., and S.L. Baron. "The Occupational Health Status of Hired Farmworkers," *Occupational Medicine: State of the Art Reviews*, 14: 6 13-35, 1999.

Washington State Housing Finance Commission (WSHFC). *A Short History of Migrant Farmworker Housing in Washington State*, 2006.

Weigel, M. Margaret, Rodrigo X. Armijos, Yolanda Posada Hall, Yolanda Ramirez, and Rubi Orozco. "The Household Food Insecurity and Health Outcomes of U.S.–Mexico Border Migrant and Seasonal Farmworkers," *Journal of Immigrant Minority Health*, 9:157–169, 2007.

GLOSSARY

Agricultural service workers—Refers to farm-related services performed on a farm or ranch on a contract or fee arrangement. This mainly includes activities performed by contract workers on fruit, vegetable, or berry operations. It also includes custom work that might require specialized equipment, veterinarian work, sheep shearing, milk testing, or other farm-related activities performed on a farm or ranch on a fee rather than hourly basis.

Annual average number of hired farmworkers—The average number of hired farmworkers employed per week during 1998.

Contract labor—Refers to contract workers who are paid by a crew leader, contractor, cooperative, or other person with a formal agreement with a farmer or rancher. Examples include pruning, weeding, or harvesting fruit and vegetable crops.

Geographic regions—Five regions using the States of the four principal Census regions and creating a fifth Southwest region with States from the South and West:

Northeast—Connecticut, Maine, Massachusetts, New Hampshire, New Jersey, New York, Pennsylvania, Rhode Island, and Vermont.

South—Alabama, Arkansas, Delaware, Florida, Georgia, Kentucky, Louisiana, Maryland, Mississippi, North Carolina, Oklahoma, South Carolina, Tennessee, Virginia, and West Virginia.

Midwest—Indiana, Illinois, Iowa, Kansas, Michigan, Minnesota, Missouri, Nebraska, North Dakota, Ohio, South Dakota, and Wisconsin.

West—Alaska, Hawaii, Idaho, Montana, Nevada, Oregon, Utah, Washington, and Wyoming.

Southwest—Arizona, California, Colorado, New Mexico, and Texas. **Crops**—Two general categories:

Field crops refer to wheat, rice, corn, soybeans, barley, dry beans, rye, sorghum, cotton, popcorn, tobacco, or similar crops.

Other crops refer to vegetables, melons, berry crops, grapes, tree nuts, citrus fruits, deciduous tree fruits, avocados, dates, figs, olives, nursery, or greenhouse crops. This category also includes potatoes, sugar crops, hay, peanuts, hops, mint, and maple syrup.

Full-time workers—Persons who usually work 35 hours or more per week. Persons working less than 35 hours per week are considered part-time.

Hired farmworkers—Employed persons who, during the survey week, did farmwork for cash wages or salary, or did not work but had farm jobs from which they were temporarily absent. Hired farmworkers include persons who manage farms for employers on a paid basis, supervisors of farmworkers, and farm and nursery workers.

Hispanic—A pan-ethnic term that encompasses people whose origins include Mexico, Central America, South America, and the Caribbean. People who self-identify as Hispanic or Latino may be of any race.

Industry—Hired farmworkers were classified according to the industry of the establishment where they worked:

Crop production—Establishments primarily engaged in producing crops, plants, vines, and trees (excluding forestry operations).

Livestock production—Establishments primarily engaged in the keeping, grazing, or feeding of livestock.

Other agricultural establishments—Establishments primarily engaged in agricultural services.

Legal status—Legal status is comprised of three categories: citizens, authorized or documented workers, and unauthorized or undocumented workers.

Citizens acquire their citizenship either by being born in the United States or by naturalizing, and thereby converting their citizenship to the United States from another country through legal processes.

Authorized workers acquire their legal status to work in the United States through legal channels such as the H-2A visa program, the Special Agricultural Workers (SAW) program, through amnesty programs such as the Immigration Reform and Control Act of 1986, as political refugees, and through other legal programs.

Unauthorized workers do not have the legal right to work in the United States, and unless they have valid tourist or student visas, they possess no right to live in the United States.

Livestock—Includes poultry, cattle, hogs, sheep, goats, and other animals raised for profit.

Median weekly earnings—The value that divides the earnings distribution into two equal parts, earnings above the median and earnings below the median. "Earnings" refers to weekly earnings the farmworker usually earns at a farm job, before deductions, and includes overtime pay or commissions.

Race—The Census Bureau defines race by dividing the population into the following groups: American Indian and Alaska Native; Asian; Black or African American; Native Hawaiian and Other Pacific Islander; and White. For the first time in 2000, the Bureau recorded numerous multi-racial categories. For the sake of brevity in this report, Native Hawaiian and Other Pacific Islanders were included in the Asian race category, and multi-racial categories were assigned their primary racial group. Race, which the Census Bureau describes as a "non-scientific socio-political construct" needs to be distinguished from ethnicity, which typically refers to "heritage, nationality group, lineage, or country of birth of the person or the person's parents or ancestors before their arrival in the United States" (U.S. Census Bureau, 2002).

Unemployed—Persons 15 years of age and older who, during the survey week, were:

1. Unemployed--on layoff; or
2. Unemployed--looking for employment.

Wage and salary workers—Persons 15 years of age and older who, during the survey week:

1. Did any work as paid employees; or
2. Were not working, but had jobs or businesses from which they were temporarily absent because of illness, bad weather, vacation, labor- management disputes, or personal reasons, whether they were paid for the time off or were seeking other jobs.

APPENDIX 1: ABOUT THE DATA

No single source provides all the necessary detail for understanding farm labor supply, demand, wages, earnings, benefits, and characteristics at the national level. Consequently, the intent of this report is to construct a coherent profile of hired farmworkers using data from the following key sources of information.

The National Agricultural Workers Survey (NAWS) collects detailed information on individual farmworkers, including legal status, critical characteristics for researchers of immigrant workers as well as farm labor. Since 1989, it has been conducted annually in three cycles of 10 to 12 weeks under contract to the Department of Labor. Its information is made available to the public via periodic research reports and a public-use data set. NAWS provides the most detailed data on the social and economic characteristics of field workers working in crop (but not livestock) production. NAWS collects data from personal interviews with between 1,518 and 3,600 randomly selected crop field workers. It does not, however, collect data on livestock farmworkers who make up an estimated 40 percent of the hired-farmworker population. It provides demographic and employment characteristics of workers, including literacy and education, family composition, earnings, assets, use of social services, employment history, and job characteristics. NAWS also collects information on migrant farmworkers – defined as workers who traveled 75 miles or more from home while looking for work or from job-to-job during the year. Not all questions have been asked in all 17 years of NAWS data collection. For this report, ERS obtained access to restricted NAWS data from the U.S. Department of Labor, which permitted analysis though 2006 as well as analysis of data not available to the general public. NAWS data through 2006 are now available from the DOL web site.

The Current Population Survey (CPS) provides employment and demographic information on the entire U.S. workforce, allowing comparative analyses between farmworkers and other occupation and industry groups. It is conducted each month by the Census Bureau for the Bureau of Labor Statistics (BLS) using a probability sample of about 57,000 households designed to represent the U.S. civilian noninstitutional population. Once selected, a household is interviewed for 4 consecutive months, dropped from the survey for 8 months, and then interviewed for a final 4 months. A fourth of the sample changes monthly. This strategy allows the Census Bureau to obtain month-to-month and year-to-year comparisons with minimal inconvenience to any one household. Because it is conducted monthly for the same households over 16 months, the survey undercounts unauthorized and foreign-born persons who migrate frequently and are reluctant to participate in formal Government questionnaires. The Census Bureau has since improved the weights used in the CPS so that total population figures and proportions match those of the decennial census and annual estimates. While totals may agree, demographic characteristics bias toward more established Hispanics with legal status.

The CPS obtains data on different topics over the course of each year. The **CPS March Supplement** provides detailed information on the labor force, employment, unemployment, and demographic characteristics. The **CPS Earnings File** contains additional information about hours worked per week and earnings collected from workers in about a quarter of CPS households (those in either their fourth or eighth month in the sample). The 2006 CPS earnings microdata file used in this report includes 12 months of data and consists of all records from the monthly samples of CPS households asked the additional questions during that time period. The data file contained information on 706,974 people, including 4,625 employed as hired farmworkers. Data comparisons in the analysis are based on differences significant at the 95 percent or higher level of confidence.

The Farm Labor Survey (FLS) provides total numbers of farmworkers obtained from farm establishments. Four times a year, the U.S. Department of Agriculture's National Agricultural Statistics Service (NASS) surveys about 14,500 farms in all States except Alaska. The survey provides quarterly estimates of the number of hired workers, the percentage of workers who are migrant, and average weekly hours worked. The FLS also provides average wage rates for hired workers by type (field, livestock, supervisor, and other) for 16 separate States and 15 regions. These figures are used by public and private entities to compute national wage indices and establish labor laws and regulations, including determining the number of replenishment workers admitted into the United States to offset domestic shortages and establishing minimum wage rates for agricultural workers.

It should be noted that "hired workers" refers to all types of workers on the farm, including bookkeepers, secretaries, and mechanics, as well as persons who pay themselves regular salaries, such as partners or corporate shareholders. Surveys answered by employers are far more likely to account for unauthorized workers than surveys administered to farmworkers themselves.

The Census of Agriculture offers the most complete geographic coverage of hired and contract farm labor use as measured by labor expenditures, and is currently the only national level data source that offers consistent farm labor information at the county and State level. Every 5 years, NASS sends a survey to U.S. farms and ranches. In 2002, the year of the most recent data available, 2.8 million questionnaires were mailed out to farms, defined as "any place from which $1,000 or more of agricultural products were produced and sold, or normally would have been sold, during the census year." The Census of Agriculture provides separate estimates of expenses for hired workers, contract labor, and specialized "custom-hire" services at the national, State, and county level. Expenditure data are reported across several identifiers, including: 3-digit Standard Industrial Classification of farms, the value of agricultural products sold, the size of farms in acres, the type of organization, and select operator characteristics. The Census of Agriculture also reports the number of hired workers, separated by whether they worked less than 150 days or 150 days or more. As with the Farm Labor Survey, the data refer to all hired workers on the farm, including those generally not considered hired farmworkers.

Agricultural Resource Management Survey (ARMS)

Conducted annually since 1985 by the Economic Research Service (ERS) and NASS, ARMS collects data to measure the financial condition (farm income sources, expenses, assets, and debts) and operating characteristics of farm businesses, the cost of producing agricultural commodities, and the well-being of farm operator households. The target population of the survey is operators associated with farm businesses representing agricultural production in the 48 contiguous States. Included in the farm operations data collected for each farm is information about cash wages paid to hired labor during the calendar year. ARMS data represent another source of information for corroborating statistics on the cost of hired farm labor across a range of farm characteristics.

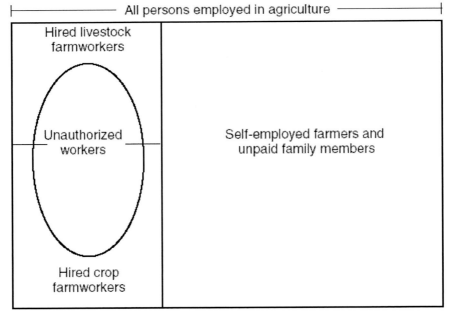

Note: Social service utilization by farmworkers occurs within 2 years of being interviewed. Unauthorized immigrants are eligible for WIC and citizen children of unauthorized immigrants are eligible for Food Stamps and Medicaid.
Source: ERS analysis of combined National Agricultural Workers Survey data, 2004-2006.

Appendix figure 1. Venn diagram of persons working in agriculture.

These data sets provide information for different subgroups within the entire population of persons employed in agriculture (app. figure 1). This latter population can be divided into two general groups: self-employed farm operators and their unpaid family members and hired farmworkers. Farmworkers may be divided according to crop and livestock production. A substantial proportion of workers in both sectors lack authorization to work in the United States.

Each of these data sources offer a different perspective on agricultural farmworkers, and it remains the challenge of researchers to synthesize this information for their specific objectives. The Census of Agriculture and FLS provide perhaps the most accurate figures on overall numbers of workers, while CPS and NAWS offer detailed characteristics of workers themselves. The latter data set includes information on legal status, while the former offers comparability with workers in other occupations.

APPENDIX 2: ESTIMATING TOTAL NUMBERS OF HIRED FARMWORKERS

Total estimates of hired farmworkers consist of two categories. The first is a cross-sectional estimate that describes, on average, the total number of hired farmworkers at any given point in time. Turnover in farmwork is considerable, and several persons may hold a single hired-farmworker position during a year. For instance, one crew of hired farmworkers planting a crop in the spring may differ from another crew of hired farmworkers harvesting that same crop in the autumn. The second category is an annual estimate of the total number of workers over the course of a year that did some type of farmwork. Cross-sectional estimates are usually derived directly from national-level survey data by Government agencies. Annual estimates, which often rely on such data, involve additional assumptions, take into account part-time work and contract labor, and are typically produced independently.

Cross-sectional national-level surveys may not accurately count hired farmworkers for several reasons. First, a substantial number of hired farmworkers are seasonal migrants who often fail to be recorded in cross-sectional surveys. Second, roughly half of all hired farmworkers are unauthorized workers according to the most reliable data available on the legal status of farmworkers. Workers without legal status fear deportation and, not surprisingly, have lower rates of participation in formal surveys (GAO, 2003). Third, surveys use different definitions of hired farmworkers. As a result, different national-level surveys yield different estimates of hired farm-workers (app. table 1).[8]

Appendix table 1. Cross-sectional estimates of total hired farmworkers, by data source

Source	Estimate	Year
Current Population Survey, March 2006 Supplement	691,000	2005
Current Population Survey Earnings File, 2006	729,000	2005
Farm Labor Survey (NASS), 2006	1,009,000	2006
Estimate by Martin (2006)	1.0-1.4 million	2006

Data from the Farm Labor Survey illustrate the degree of seasonal variation in farmworker counts, with the highest numbers registering during agriculturally productive summer months and the lowest numbers registering during winter (app. figure 2). Each annual figure from this data source represents an average of four quarterly estimates. Between 2000 and 2006, those quarterly figures ranged from a low of 759,000 (January 2005) to a high of 1,377,000 (July 2000).

Annual estimates of total hired farmworkers are typically computed using indirect methods. The Census of Agriculture, for example, reports farm labor expenditures for crop and livestock farms, but it does not provide data on the number of farm labor hours worked to allow the derivation of the number of farmworkers (by dividing the former by the latter and assuming stable wage rates).

Martin (2006) has used mixed data approaches effectively. For example, by combining data from the Census of Agriculture, CPS, FLS, and NAWS, Martin estimates there were roughly 2.5 million hired farmworkers in 2002, 1.8 million of whom worked in crops and the other 700,000 in livestock. Given the consistent decline in cross-sectional averages over the past decade, this figure has probably diminished. Based on the 2.5 million total worker figure, Martin (2006) estimates the annual number of unauthorized agricultural workers in crops and livestock between 1 and 1.4 million. Estimating the total number of persons employed in agriculture is similarly challenging. For instance, NASS, which continues to

---

[8] Hired farmworker figures from NASS's Farm Labor Survey are comprised of two groups of employees: farmworkers hired directly by farm operators and agricultural service employees. The latter group consists primarily of contract workers as well as a smaller proportion of "fee-for-service" and custom work employees. In 2006, the 1,009,000 figure included 752,000 direct hire employees and 257,000 agricultural service employees.

collect data on hired farmworkers through the FLS, discontinued counts of all other persons employed on farms (self-employed farmers and their unpaid help) in 2002. Yet in 2001, the last year it obtained quarterly data, it counted 2,047,000 self-employed farmers and their unpaid family members. The 2004 ARMS data, however, indicated 3,220,000 total farm operators, distributed among primary operators, secondary operators, spouses, and other employees (Hoppe et al., 2007). The 2002 Census of Agriculture indicated a total of 3,115,000 farm operators (Allen and Harris, 2005). Neither ARMS nor Census of Agriculture figures included hired farmworkers. The difference in estimates of total farm operators between the FLS and the other two estimates stem, in large part, from differences in measurement and definition. The Farm Labor Survey is a random-sample survey that captures, at four points each year, the number of persons employed on the farm, not all persons involved in farm production over the course of the year. Nonprimary farm operators, which according to the 2002 Census of Agriculture number about 925,000 persons, are less likely to be captured in surveys of farm operators on any given day because of their secondary role in farm operations. In contrast, the Census of Agriculture, conducted every 5 years, enumerates all farm operators who produce at least $1,000 worth of agricultural products. Procedures for this objective are more extensive than those used for quarterly FLS. In addition, the 2002 Census of Agriculture was the first to ask about secondary operators, which consequently increased the total number of farm operators from 1,911,000 in 1997 to 3,115,000 in 2002. Clearly, expanding the scope of who is considered a farm operator explains why, after decades of declines, their number increased over this period (see box, "How Definitions Alter Estimates of Total U.S. Farmworkers").

How Definitions Alter Estimates of Total U.S. Farmworkers

To illustrate how farmworker definitions can affect estimates, data from the 2006 CPS March Supplement was used to derive the 691,000 farmworkers noted. Farmworkers were defined using two criteria, one for occupation and another for industry. The March CPS data indicated that an estimated 932,000 persons held positions as managers, supervisors, or miscellaneous workers, and did so within the industries of crop production, animal production, and support activities for agriculture and forestry. This definition excludes technical occupations such as agricultural inspectors, graders, and sorters of agricultural products, and it also excludes industries such as fishing and logging.

Having narrowed occupation and industry definitions, the estimate was further refined using employment criteria. First, the calculation excluded unemployed workers and workers not in the labor force. This reduces the 932,000 figure by roughly 15 percent, to just under 800,000. Next, selfemployed persons were excluded, such as farm operators, and only wage and salary workers were retained. This reduces the 800,000 figure by an additional 13 percent to yield a final total farmworkers count of 691,000.

This figure differs substantially from the estimate by Passel (2006) of 839,000 agricultural workers that is based on less restrictive definitions and uses 2005 March CPS data. These differences illustrate the challenge of obtaining standard and comparable estimates on the number of farmworkers, even with the use of established national-scale surveys.

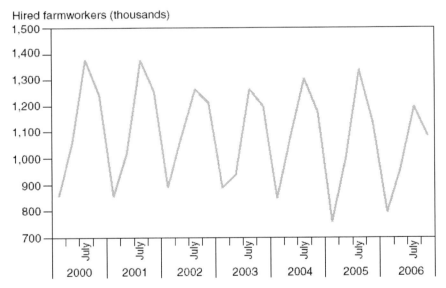

Source: Farm Labor Survey, National Agricultural Statistics Service, USDA, 2000-2006.

Appendix figure 2. Number of hired farmworkers, by quarter, 2000-2006.

APPENDIX 3: A BRIEF HISTORY OF FARM LABOR

1860s-1880s: Farming becomes a large scale industry, particularly in California. Native Americans and later Chinese are recruited to work on U.S. farms to meet a growing national demand for fruit. By 1886 in California, 7 out of every 8 farmworkers are Chinese.

1890s: In California, growing numbers of Japanese workers are recruited for agricultural work, then gradually replaced with workers from Pakistan and India.

1917-1921: The first guestworker program admits 51,000 Mexican guest-workers during World War I.

1920s: In California, growing numbers of Filipino workers and a small number of Mexican workers are recruited for agricultural work.

1924: Border Patrol established between Mexico and the United States.

1930s: Numbers of white tenant farmers and share-croppers increase during the Great Depression after many sell their own farms and begin working as migrant farmworkers.

1938: The Fair Labor Standards Act creates standards applicable to all workers and governs minimum wages, maximum hours allowable without overtime pay, child labor, and recordkeeping. Agricultural employers using less than 500 man-days of agricultural labor during any calendar quarter (six or more workers each day of the week for 13 weeks; 79 percent of all farms in 1997) are exempt from minimum wage provisions, as are all range livestock producers.

1942-1964: The Bracero Program, initiated to help alleviate wartime labor shortages, allows agricultural producers to import 4.6 million Mexican workers over 22 years for seasonal farm work. The program continues after World War II at the request of producers, but is terminated in 1964 for a variety of reasons related to flaws in the program and broader societal trends.

1947: The Federal Insecticide, Fungicide, and Rodenticide Act (FIFRA) sets risk and benefit standards for pesticide use. It was amended by the Environmental Protection Agency in 1972, 1974, and 1992.

1960s-1970s: Union activity increases among farmworkers, as does unauthorized migration and use of labor contractors.

1963: Congress passes the first Federal law regulating farm labor contractors, the Farm Labor Contractor Registration Act (FLCRA). This Act was revised 10 years later and then replaced by the current law in 1983.

1970: The Occupational Safety and Health Act (OSHA) is enacted to ensure safe and healthful working conditions for all U.S. workers.

1970s-1990s: As African Americans move into other industries, immigrants primarily from Latin America migrate toward jobs in agriculture.

1983: The Migrant and Seasonal Agricultural Worker Protection Act is enacted to provide migrant and seasonal farmworkers with protections concerning transportation, housing, pay, and working conditions. The act also requires farm labor contractors to register with the U.S. Department of Labor. Farm operators employing less than 500 man-days under the Fair Labor Standards Act of 1938 are exempt.

1986-1989: Roughly 2.7 million unauthorized workers in the United States received legal amnesty through the Immigration Reform and Control Act (IRCA) of 1986 which included a Special Agricultural Workers (SAW) legalization program for persons able to demonstrate agricultural employment prior to 1985-86. Anticipated improvements in farmworker wages and benefits failed to materialize with a rebounding ample supply of unauthorized workers, prompting many agricultural workers to seek employment in nonagricultural industries in regions outside the Southwest.

1996: The Illegal Immigration Reform and Immigrant Responsibility Act (IIRIRA) sets new guidelines for border enforcement and controls to verify eligibility for employment and social services. Border control is increased substantially, benefits available to immigrants are reduced, and a pilot program is established allowing employers and public agencies to check applicant eligibility.

Sources: Griffith and Kissam, 1995; Runyan, 2000; Martin, 2003; Martin et al., 2006.

In: Hired Farmworkers: Profile and Labor Issues   ISBN: 978-1-60741-232-8
Editor: Rea S. Berube, pp. 69-115   © 2009 Nova Science Publishers, Inc.

Chapter 2

TEMPORARY FARM LABOR: THE H-2A PROGRAM AND THE U.S. DEPARTMENT OF LABOR'S PROPOSED CHANGES IN THE ADVERSE EFFECT WAGE RATE (AEWR)[*]

Gerald Mayer

ABSTRACT

    The H-2A temporary agricultural worker program allows American agricultural employers to hire foreign workers to perform full-time temporary or seasonal work on farms in the United States. H-2A workers must be paid *at least* the highest of the adverse effect wage rate (AEWR), the prevailing wage, or the applicable federal or state minimum wage. The prevailing wage is based on state surveys funded by the U.S. Department of Labor (DOL). The AEWR is based on wage data from the Farm Labor Survey (FLS), which is conducted by the U.S. Department of Agriculture.
    On February 13, 2008, the U.S. Department of Labor (DOL) published proposed regulations that would change the way the AEWR is determined. Final action on the proposed rule is expected in November 2008. Under the rule, the AEWR would be calculated from the Occupational Employment Statistics (OES) survey, which is conducted by the Bureau of Labor Statistics of the U.S. Department of Labor and state workforce agencies. Wages from the OES survey are available at four levels of skill and experience. The four wage levels

---

[*] Excerpted from CRS Report RL34739, dated November 6, 2008.

are called Level I, Level II, Level III, and Level IV. Under the proposed rule, the AEWR could not be less than $7.25 an hour. The FLS and OES surveys cover different farm-related employers and provide different levels of detail by occupation and geographic area. An issue for Congress is the impact of the proposed change on the wages and employment of unauthorized farmworkers, H-2A workers, and U.S. workers.

Generally speaking, under the proposed rule, in most areas both the minimum AEWR of $7.25 and the OES Level I wage (for entry level workers) would be lower than the current AEWR. In some areas, however, the Level I wage would be higher than the current AEWR. On the other hand, in most areas, the OES Level IV wage (for workers with management or supervisory duties), especially for livestock workers and farm equipment operators, would be higher than the current AEWR. Compared to the current AEWR, the proposed AEWR is more likely to be lower for crop workers than for livestock workers or farm equipment operators.

In some areas, the prevailing wage could become the highest of the AEWR, prevailing wage, or minimum wage. In some areas in some states, the state minimum wage could become the highest of the three wage rates.

In areas where the proposed rule would lower the wages that employers must offer H-2A workers, the rule should create an incentive for employers to hire more H-2A, as opposed to unauthorized, workers. In areas where the rule would increase the wages that employers must offer H-2A workers, the rule would probably not create an incentive to hire more H-2A workers. On the other hand, in areas where the rule would increase the wages of H-2A workers, it should create an incentive for employers to hire more U.S. workers. However, in areas where the rule would lower the wages that employers must offer H-2A workers, it could lower the wages employers offer U.S. workers. This report will be updated as issues warrant.

INTRODUCTION

The H-2A temporary agricultural worker program allows American agricultural employers to hire foreign workers to perform full-time temporary or seasonal work on farms in the United States. H-2A workers must be paid *at least* the highest of the adverse effect wage rate (AEWR), the prevailing wage, or the applicable federal or state minimum wage. The AEWR is based on a farm labor survey conducted by the U.S. Department of Agriculture (USDA). Prevailing wages are based on state surveys funded by the U.S. Department of Labor (DOL).

On February 13, 2008, DOL published proposed regulations that would make changes in the H-2A program. The proposed rule would not change the requirement that H-2A workers must be paid at least the highest of the AEWR, prevailing wage, or applicable minimum wage. It would, however, change the way the AEWR is determined. Under the proposed rule, the AEWR would be calculated from wage data collected by the Occupational Employment Statistics (OES) survey, which is an employer survey conducted by DOL's Bureau of Labor Statistics and state workforce agencies (SWAs).[1] USDA's farm labor survey and DOL's employer survey cover different farm-related employers and provide different levels of detail by occupation and geographic area. An issue for Congress is the impact of the proposed change on the wages and employment of unauthorized farmworkers, H-2A workers, and U.S. workers.

This report begins with a description of the H-2A program. Next, the report explains how the AEWR is currently determined and how it would be calculated under the proposed regulations. Finally, the report examines some potential effects of the proposed change in the AEWR on the wages and employment of foreign and U.S. workers on U.S. farms.

THE H-2A PROGRAM

Under the H-2A program, employers may hire foreign workers to perform full-time temporary or seasonal agricultural work in the United States.[2] Temporary or seasonal employment is work that is performed during certain seasons or periods of the year or for a period of less than a year. An H-2A worker may be hired to fill either a temporary or permanent job, but the employer's need for the worker must be temporary. An employer cannot hire an H-2A worker to fill a job that is vacant because of a strike or lockout. Before they can hire foreign workers, employers must apply to DOL for a certification that qualified U.S. workers are not available and that the employment of foreign workers will not adversely affect the wages and working conditions of similarly employed U.S. workers.[3] The wages offered to U.S. workers must be at least the same as the wages offered to H-2A workers.

For workers paid a piece rate, their average hourly earnings must equal or exceed the higher of the AEWR or prevailing wage rate. If the earnings of piece rate workers fall below the higher level, the employer must supplement the workers' pay to raise it to the higher rate.

In addition to wage requirements, H-2A employers must meet minimum standards with respect to housing, transportation, meals, workers' compensation, and other requirements.[4]

Some temporary worker visas are subject to annual limits. The H-2A visa is not. From FY2000 to FY2007, the number of H-2A visas issued increased from 30,201 to 50,791.[5]

Although data are not available on the occupations of workers issued H-2A visas, information is available on the types of jobs that employers seek to fill with H-2A workers. In FY2007, DOL certified (i.e., approved) 7,491 requests for H-2A workers. Most certification applications request permission to employ more than one foreign worker. DOL certified requests to hire 89,575 H-2A workers.[6] On the basis of our review of H-2A program data, it appears that most (76.7%) of the 89,575 H- 2A workers requested were for crop production. Another 5.0% of the requests were for livestock production and 3.8% were for equipment operators.[7]

WAGE REQUIREMENTS FOR H-2A WORKERS

Employers must pay H-2A workers at least the highest of the prevailing wage, AEWR, or the applicable state or federal minimum wage.

Prevailing Wages

Prevailing wage rates are based on surveys funded by DOL and conducted by the states. The Employment and Training Administration (ETA) has established criteria for state prevailing wage surveys. A state must conduct a survey if H-2A workers were employed the previous season or if employers have requested or are expected to request H-2A workers for the current season. A state must also conduct a survey if 100 or more workers were employed during the previous season or are expected to be employed in the upcoming season. The surveys should only include U.S. workers employed in the same farm activity as H-2A workers.

Employment and wage data are collected from a sample of employers. Information provided by employers is verified through worker interviews. The prevailing wage is the wage paid to at least 40% of domestic seasonal workers or, if no single rate accounts for 40% of workers, the prevailing wage is the wage paid to workers at the 51st percentile.[8] States submit the results of their surveys to ETA.

Prevailing wages may be hourly, monthly, or piece rates. For workers paid a piece rate, the workers' average hourly earnings must equal or exceed the higher of the AEWR or prevailing wage rate. If a worker's hourly piece rate earnings fall below the higher level, the employer must supplement the worker's pay to raise it to the higher rate.[9]

The Adverse Effect Wage Rate

Current Procedures

The current AEWR is based on data from the Farm Labor Survey (FLS), which is a quarterly survey conducted by the U.S. Department of Agriculture (USDA).[10] The FLS provides estimates of the number of hired workers, average hours worked, and wages paid to workers employed on U.S. farms.[11] Hired workers include field workers, livestock workers, supervisors, administrative employees, and other workers employed directly by farmers.[12] Field and livestock workers include employees who operate farm equipment. Approximately 12,000 farms are surveyed each January, April, July, and October. The survey includes both full-time and part-time workers as well as workers who work either part-year or year-round. Wages consist of cash wages before taxes and other deductions. Wages paid on other than an hourly basis (e.g., a salary or piece rate) are converted to hourly rates. Average hourly wages are total wages by type of worker (i.e., crop, livestock, and all hired workers) divided by total hours worked. Wages do not include fringe benefits, bonuses, housing, or meals.[13]

USDA publishes annual estimates of average hourly wages for field and livestock workers in 15 regions. Separate estimates are published for California, Florida, and Hawaii. The 15 regions include 46 states. Alaska is not included in the survey. The AEWR is the weighted average hourly wage for field and livestock workers (combined) from the previous year's quarterly surveys. The AEWR is the same for each state within a region; for example, the AEWR is the same for Oregon and Washington. Similarly, the AEWR is the same for the six New England states and New York.[14] Nationwide, there may be up to 18 different adverse effect wage rates (i.e., if the rates are different for each of the 15 regions and the three states that are reported separately).

The FLS also collects information from about 600 employers who provide agricultural services to farmers (e.g., fruit or vegetable pickers supplied by a farm labor contractor) in California and Florida.[15] The USDA only publishes estimates of the average hourly wages of agricultural service workers in these two states.[16] Estimates of the hourly wages of agricultural service workers are not available for the 15 regions or Hawaii. Hence, the wages of agricultural service workers are not included in the calculation of the AEWR.

On the basis of our review of H-2A program data, in FY2007, 93.3% of the wages for the 89,575 H-2A workers requested were the regional or state AEWR. The prevailing wage applied to 4.7% of workers requested. Most prevailing wages were monthly wage rates or piece rates. See table 1.

Table 1. Type of Wage Paid, FY2007 H-2A Certifications

Type of Wage	Number of Workers	Percent of Workers
AEWR	83,576	93.3%
Prevailing wage	4,216	4.7%
Not identified	1,783	2.0%
Total	89,575	100.0%

Source: CRS analysis of H-2A certifications for FY2007. All monthly wage rates were assumed to be prevailing wages. U.S. Department of Labor, "H-2A Program Data," *Foreign Labor Certification Online Wage Library and Data Center*, available at [http://www.flcdatacenter.com/ CaseData.aspx].

The AEWRs for each state for the years 1990 through 2008 are shown in table 2. Because the state is not included in the FLS, no AEWR is published for Alaska. In Alaska, employers must pay H-2A workers at least the higher of the prevailing wage or the applicable state or federal minimum wage.[17]

A concern raised by some policymakers about the current procedures for determining the AEWR is that the FLS does not provide sufficient wage detail by area, occupation, or level of skill and experience required by employers. Currently, the AEWR applies equally to all crop workers, livestock workers, and farm equipment operators in a region or state. However, within a region or state, wages for the same occupation may vary because of differences in the cost of living or in the relative supply of or demand for workers.

Proposed Procedures

On February 13, 2008, DOL published proposed changes to current regulations for the H-2A program.[18] The proposed rule would change the way the AEWR is determined. Instead of using data from the Farm Labor Survey (FLS), the AEWR would be calculated using data from the Occupational Employment Statistics (OES) survey. Under the proposed rule, the AEWR could not be less than $7.25 an hour. According to DOL, the proposed change would better reflect the wages of farmworkers in local labor markets, as opposed to state or regional areas.[19]

Table 2. Adverse Effect Wage Rates by State, 1990-2008
(in current dollars per hour)

State [a]	1990	1991	1992	1993	1994	1995	1996	1997	1998	1999	2000	2001	2002	2003	2004	2005	2006	2007	2008
Alabama	$4.29	$4.46	$4.91	$5.04	$5.43	$5.66	$5.40	$5.92	$6.30	$6.30	$6.72	$6.83	$7.28	$7.49	$7.88	$8.07	$8.37	$8.51	$8.53
Arizona	4.61	4.87	5.17	5.37	5.52	5.80	5.87	5.82	6.08	6.42	6.74	6.71	7.12	7.61	7.54	7.63	8.00	8.27	8.70
Arkansas	4.04	4.40	4.73	4.87	5.26	5.19	5.27	5.70	5.98	6.21	6.50	6.69	6.77	7.13	7.38	7.80	7.58	8.01	8.41
California	5.90	5.81	5.90	6.11	6.03	6.24	6.26	6.53	6.87	7.23	7.27	7.56	8.02	8.44	8.50	8.56	9.00	9.20	9.72
Colorado	4.51	5.00	5.29	5.44	5.57	5.62	5.64	6.09	6.39	6.73	7.04	7.43	7.62	8.07	8.36	8.93	8.37	8.64	9.42
Connecticut	4.98	5.21	5.61	5.82	5.97	6.21	6.36	6.71	6.84	7.18	7.68	8.17	7.94	8.53	9.01	9.05	9.16	9.50	9.70
Delaware	4.89	4.93	5.39	5.81	5.92	5.81	5.97	6.26	6.33	6.84	7.04	7.37	7.46	7.97	8.52	8.48	8.95	9.29	9.70
Florida	5.16	5.38	5.68	5.91	6.02	6.33	6.54	6.36	6.77	7.13	7.25	7.66	7.69	7.78	8.18	8.07	8.56	8.56	8.82
Georgia	4.29	4.46	4.91	5.04	5.43	5.66	5.40	5.92	6.30	6.30	6.72	6.83	7.28	7.49	7.88	8.07	8.37	8.51	8.53
Hawaii	7.70	7.85	7.95	8.11	8.36	8.73	8.60	8.62	8.83	8.97	9.38	9.05	9.25	9.42	9.60	9.75	9.99	10.32	10.86
Idaho	4.49	4.79	4.94	5.25	5.59	5.57	5.76	6.01	6.54	6.48	6.79	7.26	7.43	7.70	7.69	8.20	8.47	8.76	8.74
Illinois	4.88	5.05	5.59	5.85	6.02	6.18	6.23	6.66	7.18	7.53	7.62	8.09	8.38	8.65	9.00	9.20	9.21	9.88	9.90
Indiana	4.88	5.05	5.59	5.85	6.02	6.18	6.23	6.66	7.18	7.53	7.62	8.09	8.38	8.65	9.00	9.20	9.21	9.88	9.90
Iowa	5.03	4.85	5.15	5.65	5.76	5.72	5.90	6.22	6.86	7.17	7.76	7.84	8.33	8.91	9.28	8.95	9.49	9.95	10.44
Kansas	5.17	5.20	5.36	5.78	6.03	5.99	6.29	6.55	7.01	7.12	7.49	7.81	8.24	8.53	8.83	9.00	9.23	9.55	9.90
Kentucky	4.45	4.56	5.04	5.09	5.29	5.47	5.54	5.68	5.92	6.28	6.39	6.60	7.07	7.20	7.63	8.17	8.24	8.65	9.13
Louisiana	4.04	4.40	4.73	4.87	5.26	5.19	5.27	5.70	5.98	6.21	6.50	6.69	6.77	7.13	7.38	7.80	7.58	8.01	8.41
Maine	4.98	5.21	5.61	5.82	5.97	6.21	6.36	6.71	6.84	7.18	7.68	8.17	7.94	8.53	9.01	9.05	9.16	9.50	9.70
Maryland	4.89	4.93	5.39	5.81	5.92	5.81	5.97	6.26	6.33	6.84	7.04	7.37	7.46	7.97	8.52	8.48	8.95	9.29	9.70
Massachusetts	4.98	5.21	5.61	5.82	5.97	6.21	6.36	6.71	6.84	7.18	7.68	8.17	7.94	8.53	9.01	9.05	9.16	9.50	9.70
Michigan	4.45	4.90	5.16	5.38	5.64	5.65	6.19	6.56	6.85	7.34	7.65	8.07	8.57	8.70	9.11	9.18	9.43	9.65	10.01
Minnesota	4.45	4.90	5.16	5.38	5.64	5.65	6.19	6.56	6.85	7.34	7.65	8.07	8.57	8.70	9.11	9.18	9.43	9.65	10.01
Mississippi	4.04	4.40	4.73	4.87	5.26	5.19	5.27	5.70	5.98	6.21	6.50	6.69	6.77	7.13	7.38	7.80	7.58	8.01	8.41

Missouri	5.03	4.85	5.15	5.85	5.76	5.72	5.90	6.22	6.86	7.17	7.76	7.84	8.33	8.91	9.28	8.95	9.49	9.95	10.44
Montana	4.49	4.79	4.94	5.25	5.59	5.57	5.76	6.01	6.54	6.48	6.79	7.26	7.43	7.70	7.69	8.20	8.47	8.76	8.74
Nebraska	5.17	5.20	5.36	5.78	6.03	5.99	6.29	6.55	7.01	7.12	7.49	7.81	8.24	8.53	8.83	9.00	9.23	9.55	9.90
Nevada	4.51	5.00	5.29	5.44	5.57	5.62	5.64	6.09	6.39	6.73	7.04	7.43	7.62	8.07	8.36	8.93	8.37	8.64	9.42
New Hampshire	4.98	5.21	5.61	5.82	5.97	6.21	6.36	6.71	6.84	7.18	7.68	8.17	7.94	8.53	9.01	9.05	9.16	9.50	9.70
New Jersey	4.89	4.93	5.39	5.81	5.92	5.81	5.97	6.26	6.33	6.84	7.04	7.37	7.46	7.97	8.52	8.48	8.95	9.29	9.70
New Mexico	4.61	4.87	5.17	5.37	5.52	5.80	5.87	5.82	6.08	6.42	6.74	6.71	7.12	7.61	7.54	7.63	8.00	8.27	8.70
New York	4.98	5.21	5.61	5.82	5.97	6.21	6.36	6.71	6.84	7.18	7.68	8.17	7.94	8.53	9.01	9.05	9.16	9.50	9.70
North Carolina	4.33	4.50	4.97	5.07	5.38	5.50	5.80	5.79	6.16	6.54	6.98	7.06	7.53	7.75	8.06	8.24	8.51	9.02	8.85
North Dakota	5.17	5.20	5.36	5.78	6.03	5.99	6.29	6.55	7.01	7.12	7.49	7.81	8.24	8.53	8.83	9.00	9.23	9.55	9.90
Ohio	4.88	5.05	5.59	5.85	6.02	6.18	6.23	6.66	7.18	7.53	7.62	8.09	8.38	8.65	9.00	9.20	9.21	9.88	9.90
Oklahoma	4.65	4.61	4.87	5.01	4.98	5.32	5.50	5.48	5.92	6.25	6.49	6.98	7.28	7.29	7.73	7.89	8.32	8.66	9.02
Oregon	5.42	5.69	5.94	6.31	6.51	6.41	6.82	6.87	7.08	7.34	7.64	8.14	8.60	8.71	8.73	9.03	9.01	9.77	9.94
Pennsylvania	4.89	4.93	5.39	5.81	5.92	5.81	5.97	6.26	6.33	6.84	7.04	7.37	7.46	7.97	8.52	8.48	8.95	9.29	9.70
Rhode Island	4.98	5.21	5.61	5.82	5.97	6.21	6.36	6.71	6.84	7.18	7.68	8.17	7.94	8.53	9.01	9.05	9.16	9.50	9.70
South Carolina	4.29	4.46	4.91	5.04	5.43	5.66	5.40	5.92	6.30	6.30	6.72	6.83	7.28	7.49	7.88	8.07	8.37	8.51	8.53
South Dakota	5.17	5.20	5.36	5.78	6.03	5.99	6.29	6.55	7.01	7.12	7.49	7.81	8.24	8.53	8.83	9.00	9.23	9.55	9.90
Tennessee	4.45	4.56	5.04	5.09	5.29	5.47	5.54	5.68	5.92	6.28	6.39	6.60	7.07	7.20	7.63	8.17	8.24	8.65	9.13
Texas	4.65	4.61	4.87	5.01	4.98	5.32	5.50	5.48	5.92	6.25	6.49	6.98	7.28	7.29	7.73	7.89	8.32	8.66	9.02
Utah	4.51	5.00	5.29	5.44	5.57	5.62	5.64	6.09	6.39	6.73	7.04	7.43	7.62	8.07	8.36	8.93	8.37	8.64	9.42
Vermont	4.98	5.21	5.61	5.82	5.97	6.21	6.36	6.71	6.84	7.18	7.68	8.17	7.94	8.53	9.01	9.05	9.16	9.50	9.70
Virginia	4.33	4.50	4.97	5.07	5.38	5.50	5.80	5.79	6.16	6.54	6.98	7.06	7.53	7.75	8.06	8.24	8.51	9.02	8.85

Washington	5.42	5.69	5.94	6.31	6.51	6.41	6.82	6.87	7.08	7.34	7.64	8.14	8.60	8.71	8.73	9.03	9.01	9.77	9.94
West Virginia	4.45	4.56	5.04	5.09	5.29	5.47	5.54	5.68	5.92	6.28	6.39	6.60	7.07	7.20	7.63	8.17	8.24	8.65	9.13
Wisconsin	4.45	4.90	5.16	5.38	5.64	5.65	6.19	6.56	6.85	7.34	7.65	8.07	8.57	8.70	9.11	9.18	9.43	9.65	10.01
Wyoming	4.49	4.79	4.94	5.25	5.59	5.57	5.76	6.01	6.54	6.48	6.79	7.26	7.43	7.70	7.69	8.20	8.47	8.76	8.74

Source: Compiled from data provided by the U.S. Department of Labor, Employment and Training Administration. See *Federal Register*, February 26, 2003, pp. 8929-8930; March 19, 2003, p. 13331; March 3, 2004, pp. 10063-10065; March 2, 2005, pp. 10152-10153; March 16, 2006, pp. 13633-13635; February 21, 2007, pp. 7909-7911; and February 26, 2008, pp. 10288-10290.

a. Because it is not included in the Farm Labor Survey (FLS), an AEWR is not calculated for Alaska.

Occupational Employment Statistics (OES) Survey

The OES survey is a cooperative effort between the Bureau of Labor Statistics (BLS) and the state workforce agencies (SWAs). The survey collects information from approximately 200,000 establishments each May and November and provides wage estimates for workers in 801 occupations. Wages are defined as cash wages before taxes and other deductions. The survey includes both full-time and part-time employees. Published average hourly wages are based on data collected over a three-year period from approximately 1.2 million establishments.[20] The survey does not include farmers. Instead, it includes employers involved in agricultural support activities. These are activities performed by contractors or for a fee, and include soil preparation, planting, harvesting, and management.[21] Wage data from the OES survey are available by state, metropolitan statistical area (MSA), and "balance of state" areas (BOS), which are areas that are not part of an MSA.[22]

The Four Wage Levels Calculated from the OES Survey

According to the proposed H-2A regulations, the AEWR would be based on published wage data from the Foreign Labor Certification (FLC) Data Center of DOL.[23] Using data from the OES survey, the FLC Data Center provides four levels of wages based on the skill, experience, education, and supervisory duties required for a job. Level I workers are entry-level workers who perform routine tasks that require limited exercise of judgment. Level IV workers generally have management or supervisory duties.[24] The four wage levels are currently used in the H-2B temporary nonagricultural worker program.

The Level I and IV hourly wages available from the FLC Data Center are calculated by BLS directly from OES wage data. For each occupation and area, the Level I wage is the average wage for the bottom third of the earnings distribution. The Level IV wage is the average of the top two-thirds of the earnings distribution.

The Level II and Level III wages are then calculated from the Level I and IV wages. The Consolidated Appropriations Act of 2005 (H.R. 4818, P.L. 108-447) amended the Immigration and Nationality Act (INA) to say that "Where an existing government survey has only 2 levels, 2 intermediate levels may be created by dividing by 3, the difference between the 2 levels offered, adding the quotient thus obtained to the first level and subtracting that quotient from the second level."[25]

Farm Wages from the OES Survey

The OES survey collects wage information, and the FLC Data Center provides four wage levels, for the nine farming occupations listed below. The estimated wages for farming occupations are based on data collected from employers in agricultural support activities.

- First-line supervisors or managers of farming, fishing, and forestry workers,
- Farm labor contractors,
- Agricultural inspectors,
- Animal breeders,
- Graders and sorters, agricultural products,
- Agricultural equipment operators,
- Farmworkers and laborers: crop, nursery, and greenhouse,
- Farmworkers: farm and ranch animals,
- Agricultural workers, all other.[26]

Currently, there are 363 MSAs in the United States.[27] If OES wage data were available for all MSAs, all nine farming occupations, and at four wage levels, wage data from the OES survey could provide over 13,000 adverse effect wage rates nationwide (including Alaska, but not including balance of state — that is, non-MSA — areas). The actual number of AEWRs that would be available from the OES survey may be smaller, however. If the OES survey sample for an area is too small, wage data may not be available for all farming occupations in the area.

Compared to the FLS, the OES survey provides wage information for more geographic areas and more farming occupations. In addition, the FLC Data Center provides wage rates at four levels of skill and experience. However, one of the concerns raised about the OES survey is that it does not collect wage information from farmers engaged directly in crop or livestock production. Instead, it collects wage information from employers in agricultural support activities. These employers include labor contractors who hire workers to harvest crops or tend livestock.

POTENTIAL EFFECTS OF THE PROPOSED CHANGE IN THE AEWR

DOL's proposed regulations would not change the existing requirement that H-2A workers must be paid at least the highest of the adverse effect wage rate (AEWR), the prevailing wage, or the applicable federal or state minimum wage. The proposed rule would, however, change the way the AEWR is determined. This section compares the current AEWR to the current federal and state minimum wage rates and then examines some of the potential effects of the proposed change in the way the AEWR is calculated.

Federal and State Minimum Wage Rates

The current basic federal minimum wage is $6.55 an hour. It is scheduled to rise to $7.25 an hour in July 2009.[28] The federal minimum wage applies to most agricultural employees. Exemptions apply to small agricultural employers, immediate family members, workers engaged in the production of livestock on the range, and certain hand harvesters.[29]

Several states have minimum wage rates that are higher than the federal minimum wage. When the state minimum wage is higher than the federal minimum wage, the higher state wage generally applies. As of July 24, 2008, among the 49 states with an AEWR (i.e., excluding Alaska), 23 states have a minimum wage that is higher than the federal minimum wage.

Table 3 compares the current AEWR by state with the current federal minimum wage of $6.55 and each state's minimum wage. All minimum wage rates are effective as of July 24, 2008. In each state, the current AEWR, as calculated from the FLS, is higher than either the federal or state minimum wage. In addition, in each state, the current AEWR is higher than the proposed minimum AEWR of $7.25.

Table 3. Comparisons of the Current Adverse Effect Wage Rates with Federal and State Minimum Wage Rates (as of July 24, 2008)

State	Adverse Effect Wage Rate (AEWR)	State Minimum Wage	Amount by Which the AEWR Exceeds the Federal Minimum Wage Of $6.55 an Hour	Amount by Which the AEWR Exceeds the State Minimum Wage
Alabama	$8.53	N.A.	$1.98	$8.53
Arizona	8.70	$6.90	2.15	1.80
Arkansas	8.41	6.25	1.86	2.16
California	9.72	8.00	3.17	1.72
Colorado	9.42	7.02	2.87	2.40
Connecticut	9.70	7.65	3.15	2.05
Delaware	9.70	7.15	3.15	2.55

Florida	8.82	6.79	2.27	2.03
Georgia	8.53	5.15	1.98	3.38
Hawaii	10.86	7.25	4.31	3.61
Idaho	8.74	6.55	2.19	2.19
Illinois	9.90	7.75	3.35	2.15
Indiana	9.90	6.55	3.35	3.35
Iowa	10.44	7.25	3.89	3.19
Kansas	9.90	2.65	3.35	7.25
Kentucky	9.13	6.55	2.58	2.58
Louisiana	8.41	N.A.	1.86	8.41
Maine	9.70	7.00	3.15	2.70
Maryland	9.70	6.55	3.15	3.15
Massachusetts	9.70	8.00	3.15	1.70
Michigan	10.01	7.40	3.46	2.61
Minnesota	10.01	6.15	3.46	3.86
Mississippi	8.41	N.A.	1.86	8.41
Missouri	10.44	6.65	3.89	3.79
Montana	8.74	6.55	2.19	2.19
Nebraska	9.90	6.55	3.35	3.35
Nevada	9.42	6.85	2.87	2.57
New Hampshire	9.70	6.50	3.15	3.20
New Jersey	9.70	7.15	3.15	2.55
New Mexico	8.70	6.50	2.15	2.20
New York	9.70	7.15	3.15	2.55
North Carolina	8.85	6.55	2.30	2.30
North Dakota	9.90	6.55	3.35	3.35
Ohio	9.90	7.00	3.35	2.90
Oklahoma	9.02	6.55	2.47	2.47
Oregon	9.94	7.95	3.39	1.99
Pennsylvania	9.70	7.15	3.15	2.55
Rhode Island	9.70	7.40	3.15	2.30
South Carolina	8.53	N.A.	1.98	8.53
South Dakota	9.90	6.55	3.35	3.35
Tennessee	9.13	N.A.	2.58	9.13
Texas	9.02	6.55	2.47	2.47
Utah	9.42	6.55	2.87	2.87

Table 3. (Continued).

State	Adverse Effect Wage Rate (AEWR)	State Minimum Wage	Amount by Which the AEWR Exceeds the Federal Minimum Wage Of $6.55 an Hour	Amount by Which the AEWR Exceeds the State Minimum Wage
Vermont	9.70	7.68	3.15	2.02
Virginia	8.85	6.55	2.30	2.30
Washington	9.94	8.07	3.39	1.87
West Virginia	9.13	7.25	2.58	1.88
Wisconsin	10.01	6.50	3.46	3.51
Wyoming	8.74	5.15	2.19	3.59

Source: *Federal Register*, vol. 73, no. 38, February 26, 2008, pp. 10288-10290, and the U.S. Department of Labor, *Minimum Wage Laws in the States*, July 24, 2008, available at [http://www.dol.gov/esa/minwage/america.htm]. Minimum wage coverage in some states varies by size of employer.

Note: N.A. means that a state does not have a state minimum wage.

Potential Effects of the Proposed Rule on the Wages and Employment of Farmworkers in the United States

This section examines some of the potential effects on farmworker wages and employment if DOL implements the proposed change in the way the AEWR is determined.

Preview of the Findings

Under the proposed rule, in most areas both the minimum AEWR of $7.25 and the OES Level I wage (for entry level workers) would be lower than the current AEWR. In some areas, however, the Level I wage would be higher than the current AEWR. On the other hand, in most areas, the Level III and IV OES wages for livestock workers and farm equipment operators would be higher than the current AEWR. Compared to the current AEWR, the proposed AEWR is more likely to be lower for crop workers than for livestock workers or farm equipment operators.

In some areas, the prevailing wage could become the highest of the AEWR, prevailing wage, or minimum wage. In some areas in some states, the state minimum wage could become the highest of the three wage rates.

In areas where the proposed rule would lower the wages that employers must offer H-2A workers, the rule should create an incentive for employers to hire more H-2A, as opposed to unauthorized, workers. In areas where the rule would increase the wages that employers must offer H-2A workers, the rule would probably not create an incentive to hire more H-2A workers. On the other hand, in areas where the rule would increase the wages of H-2A workers, it should create an incentive for employers to hire more U.S. workers. However, in areas where the rule would lower the wages that employers must offer H-2A workers, it could lower the wages employers offer U.S. workers.

Methodology and Assumptions

In order to analyze the potential effects of the proposed rule on the wages and employment of farmworkers, it would be necessary to compare the AEWR under current procedures with the AEWR under the proposed rule. This section uses administrative data from employer requests for H- 2A workers, OES wage data from the FLC Data Center, and prevailing wage data from ETA to analyze the potential impact of the proposed rule.

The analysis compares the current AEWR for crop and livestock workers (combined), as calculated from the FLS, with the four wage levels of three occupations from the OES survey: (1) farmworkers and laborers: crop, nursery, and greenhouse production, (2) farmworkers: farm and ranch animals, and (3) equipment operators. It is assumed that, under the proposed rule, these three occupations would be used to determine the AEWR for crop workers, livestock workers, and farm equipment operators.

The analysis also compares the hourly AEWR under the proposed rule with hourly prevailing wage for the same area and occupation.

The analysis is based on labor certifications for five states. These states were chosen because they are the five top states in terms of the number of H-2A workers requested in FY2007. Together, the five states accounted for 43.7% of the H-2A workers requested. The states are North Carolina (17.9%), Georgia, (8.0%), Louisiana (6.1%), Florida (6.0%), and Kentucky (5.7%).

Wage data from the OES survey are available by metropolitan statistical area (MSA) and areas that are called "balance of state" (BOS), which are areas that are not part of an MSA. At the FLC Data Center, these areas are called "BLS areas." For each state, the BLS areas encompass all of the counties in a state. OES wage data can be retrieved by county or BLS area.[30] If the OES sample is sufficiently large, wage rates are available at four levels of skill and experience for each farming occupation in each BLS area.

The analysis presented here compares the current AEWR with the proposed minimum AEWR of $7.25, the OES Level I, II, III, and IV wages, the prevailing wage, and state minimum wage rates. Under the proposed rule, the actual wage that would apply to an individual worker would depend on the occupation and the level of skill and experience required by an employer for the job. Thus, any of the four OES wage levels, the prevailing wage, or the minimum wage could become the highest of the wage rates that employers must offer to H-2A workers. The discussion below of findings and the analysis of the potential effects of the proposed rule highlight workers who would be paid the minimum $7.25 AEWR or the OES Level I wage. More emphasis is placed on these workers because it is assumed that the majority of H-2A workers are entry-level workers.

Findings

The results of the analysis of the effect of the proposed rule on the AEWR are summarized in tables 4 through 7. For each of the five states chosen, table 4 shows the number of BLS areas where the OES Level I wage is less than or equal to the current AEWR (column 3) and the number of areas where the proposed Level I AEWR is higher than the current AEWR (column 6). The number of areas where the proposed AEWR would be less than or equal to the current AEWR is separated into two groups: Column 4 shows the number of BLS areas where the proposed minimum AEWR of $7.25 is lower than the current AEWR and column 5 shows the number of areas where the OES Level I wage is more than $7.25 an hour, but less than or equal to the current AEWR.

Tables 5 through 7 are similar to table 4, except they compare the current AEWR to the OES Levels II, III, and IV wages for each state, area, and occupation. Tables 13 though 16 in the Appendix show the prevailing wage rates for North Carolina, Georgia, Florida, and Kentucky. No prevailing wage rates are currently available for Louisiana.

In general, the results show the following.

- In most areas, the $7.25 minimum AEWR and the OES Level I wage for crop workers, livestock workers, and farm equipment operators are lower than the current AEWR.[31] For example, for cropworkers in North Carolina, the OES Level I wage is lower than the current AEWR in 18 of 19 BLS areas (compare columns 2 and 3 in table 4).
- In many areas, the $7.25 minimum AEWR is lower than the current AEWR. For example, in Georgia, the $7.25 minimum AEWR is lower than the current AEWR in 15 of 19 BLS areas. Assuming the $7.25 wage would not be adjusted

for inflation (as wages rise due to inflation, increased productivity, or both), as time passes the $7.25 wage would apply to fewer areas.
- The minimum $7.25 AEWR and the OES Level I wage are more likely to be lower than the current AEWR for crop workers than for livestock workers or farm equipment operators. For example, for crop workers, the $7.25 minimum AEWR is lower than the current AEWR in 51 of the 83 total BLS areas represented in table 4 —compared to livestock workers in 27 areas and farm equipment operators in 24 areas.
- In some areas, the OES Level I wage is higher than the current AEWR. For example, for equipment operators, the OES Level I wage is higher than the current AEWR in 22 of the 83 BLS areas shown in table 4. Half of these 22 areas are in Kentucky. (See column 6.)
- In most areas, the Level III and IV OES wages for livestock workers and farm equipment operators are higher than the current AEWR. For example, the Level IV wage for equipment operators is higher than the current AEWR in all 83 wage areas shown in table 7. For livestock workers, the Level IV wage is higher than the current AEWR in 80 of 83 areas. On the other hand, in 13 of 83 areas, the Level IV wage for crop workers is lower than the current AEWR.
- In some areas, the prevailing wage could become the highest of the AEWR, the prevailing wage, or the applicable minimum wage. For example, in Greenville, North Carolina, the prevailing wage for tobacco harvesters is $7.50 an hour. (See table 13.) This is less than the current AEWR of $8.85 but higher than the proposed minimum AEWR of $7.25 or the Level I, II, or III OES wages for crop workers in the Greenville MSA. Similarly, in Brunswick and Valdosta (i.e., southern), Georgia, the prevailing wage of $8.00 an hour for tractor drivers is less than the current AEWR of $8.53 but higher than the Level I or II OES wages for equipment operators. (See tables 9 and 14.)
- Finally, in some areas in some states, the state minimum wage could become the highest wage that employers must offer to H-2A workers. In none of the five states studied here is the state minimum wage higher than the $7.25 minimum AEWR. But, as of July 24, 2008, nine states have minimum wages that are higher than the minimum $7.25 AEWR. Whether the state minimum wage would apply to an H-2A worker would depend on whether it is higher than the prevailing wage or the OES wage for the job.

Comparison of the AEWR Based on the FLS Versus OES Survey

The current AEWR may overestimate the wages of crop workers and underestimate the wages of livestock workers and farm equipment operators. Except for equipment operators in Kentucky, the $7.25 minimum AEWR and the OES Level I wage for the three occupations shown in table 4 are generally lower than the current AEWR. For example, in Georgia, the OES Level I wage for livestock workers is lower than the current AEWR in all 19 BLS areas (compare columns 2 and 3). In Florida, the Level I wage for equipment operators is lower than the current AEWR in 17 of 20 BLS areas.

In general, the OES Level II wage for crop workers is also lower than the current AEWR. See table 5. This is not the case, however, for livestock workers or farm equipment operators. With some exceptions (e.g., livestock workers in parts of Louisiana and Kentucky and equipment operators in parts of Georgia), the Level II wages for livestock workers and farm equipment operators are generally higher than the current AEWR. The same is true for both the Level III and Level IV wages. Thus, the proposed rule may have more of an adverse effect on the wages of crop workers than on the wages of either livestock workers or equipment operators.

Potential Effects of the Proposed Regulation on the Wages and Employment of Farmworkers

If the proposed rule is implemented as written, its effect on the wages and employment of farmworkers would depend on a number of factors. First, the rule may either raise or lower the wages employers must offer H-2A workers. Second, the effect of the rule may vary by area and occupation. The effect on the wages and employment of crop workers may be different from the effect on livestock workers or farm equipment operators. The effect may be different in labor markets where local wages are above or below the current AEWR. Finally, the effect of the rule may be different for three groups of workers: unauthorized farmworkers, H-2A workers, and U.S. workers.[32]

Effect of the Proposed Rule on Wages

Under the proposed rule, employers would have to offer H-2A workers at least the highest of the minimum AEWR of $7.25, the OES wage level that applies to the job, the prevailing wage, or the state minimum wage. (Under current law, the federal minimum wage is not scheduled to increase to more than $7.25 an hour.) Depending on local wages for the occupation, skill, and experience that employers require for a job, the wage that employers would have to offer H-2A workers under the proposed rule may be lower or higher than the wage that employers must offer under current regulations. Under the proposed rule, for employers who hire mainly entry level workers, the minimum AEWR of $7.25, the OES Level I or Level II wage, the prevailing wage, or the state minimum wage would likely apply. Nevertheless, for some occupations in some areas, even the Level I or Level II wage would be higher than the current AEWR.

The current AEWR is higher than the state minimum wage in all states. On the other hand, as of July 24, 2008, the state minimum wage is greater than the minimum AEWR of $7.25 in nine states. Whether the state minimum wage would apply to H-2A workers in these states would depend on whether it is higher than either the proposed AEWR or the prevailing wage.

For those H-2A workers who qualify for Level III or Level IV OES wages, the AEWR would likely be higher than the wage that applies under current regulations. In most areas, the Level III and IV wages for livestock workers and farm equipment operators are higher than the current AEWR. On the other hand, in some areas, even the Level III or Level IV wage, especially for crop workers, would be lower than the current AEWR.

Effect of the Proposed Rule on Employment

The effect of the proposed rule on the demand for H-2A versus unauthorized workers may vary depending on whether the rule lowers or raises the wages employers must offer H-2A workers.

In FY2007, 50,791 H-2A temporary agricultural worker visas were issued. At the end of FY2007, an estimated 1.1 million hired farmworkers were employed on U.S. farms and ranches.[33] According to findings from the National Agricultural Workers Survey (NAWS), as many as half of crop workers on U.S. farms are not authorized to work in the United States.[34] Thus, the available data suggest that U.S. farmers and farm labor contractors employ more unauthorized crop workers than H-2A workers.

Under the proposed rule, the AEWR should more closely reflect the wages of farmworkers in local labor markets. In labor markets with a large concentration of unauthorized farmworkers, wage data from the OES survey may, to some extent, reflect the wages paid to unauthorized workers.[35] For employers who hire mainly entry-level workers, the proposed rule may lower the wages employers must offer H-2A workers and could create an incentive for employers to hire more legal, as opposed to unauthorized, foreign farmworkers. On the other hand, the rule may not increase the incentive for employers to hire H-2A workers if it raises the wages employers must offer H-2A workers.

Table 4. The Number of BLS Areas Where the Proposed AEWR, Using OES Level I Wage Rates, Would be Less Than or Greater Than the Current AEWR: A Comparison of Five States

State (1)	Number of BLS Areas (2)	Number of BLS Areas Where the Proposed AEWR Would Be Less Than the Current AEWR			Number of BLS Areas Where the Proposed AEWR Would Be Greater Than the Current AEWR (6)
		Total (3)	Number of Areas Where the $7.25 Minimum AEWR Would Apply (4)	Number of Areas Where the Proposed AEWR Would Be Greater Than $7.25 but Less Than or Equal to the Current AEWR (5)	
North Carolina	19	18	11	7	1
Georgia	19	18	15	3	1
Louisiana	12	12	8	4	0
Florida	20	18	10	8	2
Kentucky	13 [a]	12	7	5	0
North Carolina	19	16	0	16	3
Georgia	19	19	7	12	0
Louisiana	12	11	10 [b]	1	1
Florida	20	18	2	16	2
Kentucky	13	11	8	3	2
Equipment Operators					
North Carolina	19	16	8	8	3
Georgia	19	16	15	1	3
Louisiana	12	10	0	10	2
Florida	20	17	1	16	3
Kentucky	13	2	0	2 [c]	11

Source: CRS calculations based on the assumptions outlined in the text of this report. The Level I OES wage rates by state and BLS area are shown in the Appendix.

[a] For one of the BLS areas in Kentucky, no OES data for crop workers are available for the period.

[b] For one of the BLS areas in Louisiana, the OES Level I wage for livestock workers is $7.25, the same as the floor for the proposed AEWR.

[c] For one of the BLS areas in Kentucky, the OES Level I wage for equipment operators is $9.13, the same as the current AEWR.

Table 5. The Number of BLS Areas Where the Proposed AEWR, Using OES Level II Wage Rates, Would be Less Than or Greater Than the Current AEWR: A Comparison of Five States

State (1)	Number of BLS Areas (2)	Number of BLS Areas Where the Proposed AEWR Would Be Less Than the Current AEWR			Number of BLS Areas Where the Proposed AEWR Would Be Greater Than the Current AEWR (6)
		Total (3)	Number of Areas Where the $7.25 Minimum AEWR Would Apply (4)	Number of Areas Where the Proposed AEWR Would Be Greater Than $7.25 but Less Than or Equal to the Current AEWR (5)	
North Carolina	19	14	4	10	5
Georgia	19	17	5	12	2
Louisiana	12	7	2	5	5
Florida	20	11	0	11	9
Kentucky	13 [a]	10	0	10	2
North Carolina	19	4	0	4	15
Georgia	19	4	0	4	15
Louisiana	12	9	0	9	3
Florida	20	3	0	3	17
Kentucky	13	10	1	9	3
Equipment Operators					
North Carolina	19	5	0	5	14
Georgia	19	14	2	12	5
Louisiana	12	0	0	0	12
Florida	20	2	0	2	18
Kentucky	13	0	0	0	13

Sources: CRS calculations based on the assumptions outlined in the text of this report. The Level II OES wage rates by state, BLS area, and wage level are shown in the Appendix.

[a] For one of the BLS areas in Kentucky, no OES data for crop workers are available for the period.

Table 6. The Number of BLS Areas Where the Proposed AEWR, Using OES Level III Wage Rates, Would be Less Than or Greater Than the Current AEWR: A Comparison of Five States

State (1)	Number of BLS Areas (2)	Number of BLS Areas Where the Proposed AEWR Would Be Less Than the Current AEWR				Number of BLS Areas Where the Proposed AEWR Would Be Greater Than the Current AEWR (6)
		Total (3)	Number of Areas Where the $7.25 Minimum AEWR Would Apply (4)	Number of Areas Where the Proposed AEWR Would Be Greater Than $7.25 but Less Than or Equal to the Current AEWR (5)		
North Carolina	19	9	0	9		10
Georgia	19	8	0	8		11
Louisiana	12	2	1	1		10
Florida	20	6	0	6		14
Kentucky	13 [a]	6	0	6		6
North Carolina	19	0	0	0		19
Georgia	19	2	0	2		17
Louisiana	12	3	0	3		9
Florida	20	0	0	0		20
Kentucky	13	6	0	6		7
Equipment Operators						
North Carolina	19	0	0	0		19
Georgia	19	4	0	4 [b]		15
Louisiana	12	0	0	0		12
Florida	20	0	0	0		20
Kentucky	13	0	0	0		13

Source: CRS calculations based on the assumptions outlined in the text of this report. The Level III OES wage rates by state and BLS area are shown in the Appendix.

[a] For one of the BLS areas in Kentucky, no OES data for crop workers are available for the period.

[b] For one of the BLS areas in Georgia, the OES Level III wage for equipment operators is $8.53, the same as the current AEWR.

Table 7. The Number of BLS Areas Where the Proposed AEWR, Using OES Level IV Wage Rates, Would be Less Than or Greater Than the Current AEWR: A Comparison of Five States

State (1)	Number of BLS Areas (2)	Number of BLS Areas Where the Proposed AEWR Would Be Less Than the Current AEWR			Number of BLS Areas Where the Proposed AEWR Would Be Greater Than the Current AEWR (6)
		Total (3)	Number of Areas Where the $7.25 Minimum AEWR Would Apply (4)	Number of Areas Where Proposed AEWR Would Be Greater Than $7.25 but Less Than or Equal to Current AEWR	
Farmworkers and Laborers: Crop, Nursery, and Greenhouse					
North	19	6	0	6	13
Georgia	19	5	0	5	14
Louisiana	12	1	1	0	11
Florida	20	1	0	1	19
Kentucky	13[a]	0	0	0	12
Farmworkers: Farm and Ranch Animals					
North	19	0	0	0	19
Georgia	19	0	0	0	19
Louisiana	12	1	0	1	11
Florida	20	0	0	0	20
Kentucky	13	2	0	2	11
Equipment Operators					
North	19	0	0	0	19
Georgia	19	0	0	0	19
Louisiana	12	0	0	0	12
Florida	20	0	0	0	20
Kentucky	13	0	0	0	13

Sources: CRS calculations based on the assumptions outlined in the text of this report. The Level IV OES wage rates by state, BLS area, and wage level are shown in the Appendix.

[a] For one of the BLS areas in Kentucky, no OES data for crop workers are available for the period.

Similarly, the effect of the proposed rule on the employment of U.S. workers may depend on whether it raises or lowers the wages of foreign, as opposed to U.S., workers. The relative cost of benefits may also affect the demand for foreign and

U.S. workers. Although U.S. workers are entitled to the same benefits as H-2A workers, employer costs for housing and transportation may be greater for H-2A than U.S. workers (e.g., if U.S. workers live within commuting distance of a job).[36] Thus, the effect of the proposed rule on the employment of U.S. workers may depend on how the rule changes the relative cost (i.e., wages and benefits) of foreign versus U.S. workers.

Other factors may also affect the relative supply of or demand for foreign farmworkers, including increased enforcement of U.S. immigration law and changes in economic conditions in the United States and elsewhere. It may be difficult, however, to separate the effects of these, and other, changes from the effect of the proposed rule on hourly wages.

APPENDIX

Tables 8 through 12 show the four wage levels calculated from the OES survey for each of the BLS areas in five states: North Carolina, Georgia, Louisiana, Florida, and Kentucky. BLS areas consist of MSAs and areas within a state that are not part of an MSA. BLS areas encompass all of the counties in a state. The wage rates are effective for the period July 2008 through June 2009.

Tables 13 though 16 show the prevailing wage rates for North Carolina, Georgia, Florida, and Kentucky. No prevailing wage rates are currently available for Louisiana. The prevailing wage rates apply to work scheduled for the years 2008 to 2009.

Table 8. The Four Hourly Wage Levels from the OES Survey for the State of North Carolina, Effective July 2008 Through June 2009

BLS area	Farmworkers and Laborers: Crop, Nursery, and Greenhouse				Farmworkers: Farm and Ranch Animals				Equipment Operators			
	Level I	Level II	Level III	Level IV	Level I	Level II	Level III	Level IV	Level I	Level II	Level III	Level IV
Asheville	$10.68	$11.07	$11.46	$11.85	$7.69	$8.47	$9.26	$10.04	6.97	8.58	10.19	11.80
Balance of State (BOS) 1	6.95	7.26	7.57	7.88	7.90	8.94	9.99	11.03	6.71	8.15	9.60	11.04
Balance of State (BOS) 2	6.76	7.13	7.51	7.88	8.91	9.64	10.38	11.11	8.13	9.37	10.61	11.85
Balance of State (BOS) 3	6.78	7.70	8.61	9.53	8.38	8.75	9.12	9.49	8.18	9.84	11.49	13.15
Balance of State (BOS) 4	8.32	9.44	10.57	11.69	8.18	8.65	9.12	9.59	10.26	12.80	15.33	17.87
Burlington	7.74	8.62	9.51	10.39	8.42	8.81	9.20	9.59	6.97	8.58	10.19	11.80
Charlotte-Gastonia-Concord	7.37	8.44	9.51	10.58	8.00	8.49	8.99	9.48	6.97	8.58	10.19	11.80
Durham	6.77	7.50	8.23	8.96	8.23	9.14	10.05	10.96	8.18	9.66	11.13	12.61
Fayetteville	7.96	8.42	8.87	9.33	8.12	8.90	9.67	10.45	8.15	9.44	10.72	12.01
Goldsboro	6.82	8.03	9.24	10.45	8.54	9.48	10.42	11.36	8.15	9.64	11.14	12.63

BLS area	Farmworkers and Laborers: Crop, Nursery, and Greenhouse				Farmworkers: Farm and Ranch Animals				Equipment Operators			
	Level I	Level II	Level III	Level IV	Level I	Level II	Level III	Level IV	Level I	Level II	Level III	Level IV
Greensboro-High Point	7.57	8.21	8.86	9.50	8.40	9.12	9.84	10.56	8.15	9.46	10.78	12.09
Greenville	6.79	7.13	7.46	7.80	8.47	9.54	10.60	11.67	6.88	8.35	9.81	11.28
Hickory-Lenior-Morgantown	8.51	9.60	10.68	11.77	8.17	8.54	8.92	9.29	10.26	12.80	15.33	17.87
Jacksonville	6.79	7.16	7.53	7.90	8.92	9.70	10.47	11.25	6.95	8.40	9.84	11.29
Raleigh-Cary	8.05	8.82	9.59	10.36	7.62	9.28	10.94	12.60	6.91	8.39	9.88	11.36
Rocky Mount	6.79	7.32	7.85	8.38	7.29	9.57	11.85	14.13	6.88	8.41	9.93	11.46
Virginia Beach-Norfolk-Newport News	6.52	7.35	8.18	9.01	7.94	8.67	9.41	10.14	7.94	10.08	12.23	14.37
Wilmington	6.76	7.14	7.52	7.90	8.91	9.64	10.38	11.11	8.13	9.37	10.61	11.85
Winston-Salem	6.69	7.42	8.16	8.89	8.17	8.54	8.92	9.29	10.26	12.57	14.89	17.20

Source: U.S. Department of Labor, Foreign Labor Certification Data Center, *Online Wage Library*, available at [http://www.flcdatacenter.com/OesWizardStart.aspx].

Note: As a reminder, the AEWR for North Carolina is $8.85 an hour (see table 1). Also, the proposed AEWR would be based on wage data from the OES survey, but it could not be less than $7.25 an hour.

Table 9. The Four Hourly Wage Levels from the OES Survey for the State of Georgia, Effective July 2008 Through June 2009

BLS area	Farmworkers and Laborers: Crop, Nursery, and Greenhouse				Farmworkers: Farm and Ranch Animals				Equipment Operators			
	Level I	Level II	Level III	Level IV	Level I	Level II	Level III	Level IV	Level I	Level II	Level III	Level IV
Albany	$6.48	$7.30	$8.12	$8.94	$7.48	$8.80	$10.13	$11.45	$6.39	$8.17	$9.94	$11.72
Athens-Clarke County	8.29	8.98	9.66	10.35	7.35	9.18	11.01	12.84	6.32	8.14	9.95	11.77
Atlanta-Sandy Springs-Marietta	6.59	7.84	9.09	10.34	8.01	9.49	10.97	12.45	9.35	11.32	13.30	15.27
Augusta-Richmond County	6.35	8.50	10.64	12.79	7.18	9.30	11.41	13.53	7.02	9.00	10.99	12.97
Balance of State (BOS) 1	6.28	7.71	9.13	10.56	7.81	9.56	11.31	13.06	6.33	8.45	10.57	12.69
Balance of State (BOS) 2	6.45	7.31	8.16	9.02	7.82	8.61	9.41	10.20	6.34	8.24	10.14	12.04
Balance of State (BOS) 3	6.45	6.85	7.25	7.65	6.78	7.41	8.03	8.66	6.29	7.16	8.04	8.91
Balance of State (BOS) 4	6.48	6.99	7.50	8.01	7.36	8.70	10.05	11.39	6.40	7.47	8.53	9.60
Brunswick	8.54	9.38	10.23	11.07	7.19	8.57	9.95	11.33	6.39	7.48	8.57	9.66
Chattanooga, Tennessee-Georgia	7.34	8.07	8.81	9.54	6.39	7.84	9.28	10.73	8.32	9.90	11.49	13.07
Columbus, Georgia-Alabama	7.68	8.37	9.06	9.75	7.31	8.77	10.22	11.68	11.38	12.73	14.07	15.42
Dalton	6.74	7.81	8.87	9.94	7.60	9.32	11.05	12.77	6.35	8.18	10.01	11.84

BLS area	Farmworkers and Laborers: Crop, Nursery, and Greenhouse				Farmworkers: Farm and Ranch Animals				Equipment Operators			
	Level I	Level II	Level III	Level IV	Level I	Level II	Level III	Level IV	Level I	Level II	Level III	Level IV
Gainesville	6.58	7.83	9.09	10.34	8.09	9.77	11.45	13.13	6.35	8.18	10.01	11.84
Hinesville-Fort Stewart	6.47	6.98	7.49	8.00	6.90	8.09	9.29	10.48	6.34	7.35	8.36	9.37
Macon	6.58	7.81	9.05	10.28	7.76	9.26	10.75	12.25	11.68	12.98	14.28	15.58
Rome	6.58	7.82	9.07	10.31	7.09	8.96	10.82	12.69	6.35	8.18	10.01	11.84
Savannah	6.45	6.88	7.32	7.75	6.78	7.41	8.03	8.66	6.29	7.20	8.10	9.01
Valdosta	6.43	7.01	7.60	8.18	7.36	8.67	9.99	11.30	6.40	7.47	8.53	9.60
Warner Robins	6.46	7.37	8.27	9.18	7.78	8.75	9.71	10.68	6.35	8.18	10.01	11.84

Source: U.S. Department of Labor, Foreign Labor Certification Data Center, *Online Wage Library*, available at [http://www.flcdatacenter.com/OesWizardStart.aspx].

Note: As a reminder, the AEWR for Georgia is $8.53 an hour (see table 1). Also, the proposed AEWR would be based on wage data from the OES survey, but it could not be less than $7.25 an hour.

Table 10. The Four Hourly Wage Levels from the OES Survey for the State of Louisiana, Effective July 2008 Through June 2009

BLS area	Farmworkers and Laborers: Crop, Nursery, and Greenhouse				Farmworkers: Farm and Ranch Animals				Equipment Operators			
	Level I	Level II	Level III	Level IV	Level I	Level II	Level III	Level IV	Level I	Level II	Level III	Level IV
Alexandria	$8.29	$9.09	$9.88	$10.68	$6.47	$7.38	$8.29	$9.20	$8.20	$8.75	$9.30	$9.85
Baton Rouge	6.31	7.55	8.79	10.03	6.78	7.80	8.81	9.83	8.18	8.74	9.29	9.85
Balance of State (BOS) 1	6.90	8.03	9.17	10.30	7.25	8.76	10.28	11.79	8.63	10.15	11.68	13.20
Balance of State (BOS) 2	8.09	9.82	11.55	13.28	6.47	7.38	8.29	9.20	8.22	8.73	9.24	9.75
Balance of State (BOS) 3	6.23	6.99	7.75	8.51	6.80	8.05	9.29	10.54	8.20	8.65	9.09	9.54
Balance of State (BOS) 4	6.38	6.65	6.91	7.18	6.88	7.99	9.11	10.22	8.36	10.47	12.59	14.70
Houma-Bayou Cane-Thibodaux	6.40	7.96	9.53	11.09	7.93	9.67	11.42	13.16	8.20	8.75	9.30	9.85
Lafayette	6.35	7.48	8.60	9.73	6.81	7.27	7.74	8.20	8.20	8.75	9.30	9.85
Lake Charles	6.46	7.97	9.49	11.00	6.53	7.49	8.46	9.42	8.20	8.75	9.30	9.85
Monroe	7.85	8.72	9.60	10.47	7.03	8.21	9.39	10.57	8.20	8.65	9.09	9.54
New Orleans-Metairie-Kenner	6.97	8.61	10.25	11.89	10.29	11.59	12.90	14.20	8.88	10.48	12.07	13.67

BLS area	Farmworkers and Laborers: Crop, Nursery, and Greenhouse				Farmworkers: Farm and Ranch Animals				Equipment Operators			
	Level I	Level II	Level III	Level IV	Level I	Level II	Level III	Level IV	Level I	Level II	Level III	Level IV
Shreveport-Bossier City	7.40	8.83	10.25	11.68	6.81	8.24	9.67	11.10	8.22	8.66	9.09	9.53

Source: U.S. Department of Labor, Foreign Labor Certification Data Center, *Online Wage Library*, available at [http://www.flcdatacenter.com/OesWizardStart.aspx].

Note: As a reminder, the AEWR for Louisiana is $8.41 an hour (see Table 1). Also, the proposed AEWR would be based on wage data from the OES survey, but it could not be less than $7.25 an hour.

Table 11. The Four Hourly Wage Levels from the OES Survey for the State of Florida, Effective July 2008 Through June 2009

BLS area	Farmworkers and Laborers: Crop, Nursery, and Greenhouse				Farmworkers: Farm and Ranch Animals				Equipment Operators			
	Level I	Level II	Level III	Level IV	Level I	Level II	Level III	Level IV	Level I	Level II	Level III	Level IV
Balance of State (BOS) 1	$9.11	$10.87	$12.63	$14.39	$8.23	$9.94	$11.6	$13.37	$9.75	$11.31	$12.87	$14.43
Balance of State (BOS) 2	7.24	8.71	10.19	11.66	8.03	9.98	11.93	13.88	7.85	9.46	11.06	12.67
Balance of State (BOS) 3	7.08	7.63	8.19	8.74	7.08	8.07	9.06	10.05	8.22	10.16	12.10	14.04
Cape Coral-Fort Myers	7.06	8.00	8.94	9.88	7.09	8.19	9.30	10.40	7.25	8.83	10.40	11.98
Deltona-Daytona Beach-Ormond Beach	6.96	7.60	8.23	8.87	7.78	9.21	10.65	12.08	7.70	9.24	10.79	12.33
Fort Lauderdale-Pompano Beach-Deerfield Beach	7.13	7.74	8.35	8.96	9.14	10.57	11.99	13.42	7.35	8.81	10.26	11.72
Fort Walton Beach-Crestview-Destin	8.70	9.87	11.05	12.22	8.23	9.94	11.66	13.37	9.62	11.58	13.55	15.51
Gainesville	7.17	7.92	8.66	9.41	7.86	9.40	10.94	12.48	8.16	9.59	11.01	12.44
Jacksonville	7.71	9.07	10.43	11.79	7.99	9.76	11.52	13.29	8.16	9.21	10.26	11.31
Lakeland	7.22	8.14	9.07	9.99	7.48	9.17	10.85	12.54	9.13	10.48	11.84	13.19
Miami-Miami Beach-Kendall	7.07	7.99	8.91	9.83	8.04	9.41	10.77	12.14	7.90	9.28	10.67	12.05
Naples-Marco Island	7.39	7.98	8.56	9.15	7.37	8.68	9.98	11.29	7.21	8.09	8.98	9.86
Ocala	7.41	8.95	10.50	12.04	7.85	9.22	10.58	11.95	7.70	9.24	10.79	12.33
Orlando-Kissimmee	7.89	9.56	11.22	12.89	7.54	8.91	10.29	11.66	8.60	10.33	12.06	13.79
Palm Bay-Melbourne-Titusville	8.45	9.68	10.91	12.14	7.45	8.85	10.25	11.65	7.70	9.24	10.79	12.33

BLS area	Farmworkers and Laborers: Crop, Nursery, and Greenhouse				Farmworkers: Farm and Ranch Animals				Equipment Operators			
	Level I	Level II	Level III	Level IV	Level I	Level II	Level III	Level IV	Level I	Level II	Level III	Level IV
Panama City-Lynn Haven	7.13	8.05	8.96	9.88	8.23	9.94	11.66	13.37	7.70	9.24	10.79	12.33
Pensacola-Ferry Pass-Brent	8.74	9.92	11.11	12.29	8.23	9.94	11.66	13.37	7.70	9.24	10.79	12.33
Port St. Lucie-Fort Pierce	8.63	9.61	10.59	11.57	9.29	10.72	12.15	13.58	8.57	10.17	11.77	13.37
Punta Gorda	7.08	7.77	8.45	9.14	7.47	9.22	10.97	12.72	8.19	10.11	12.04	13.96
Sarasota-Bradenton-Venice	10.11	11.73	13.35	14.97	7.46	9.17	10.87	12.58	7.46	9.17	10.87	12.58

Source: U.S. Department of Labor, Foreign Labor Certification Data Center, *Online Wage Library*, available at [http://www.flcdatacenter.com/OesWizardStart.aspx].

Note: As a reminder, the AEWR for Florida is $8.82 an hour (see table 1). Also, the proposed AEWR would be based on wage data from the OES survey, but it could not be less than $7.25 an hour.

Table 12. The Four Hourly Wage Levels from the OES Survey for the State of Kentucky, Effective July 2008 Through June 2009

BLS area	Farmworkers and Laborers: Crop, Nursery, and Greenhouse				Farmworkers: Farm and Ranch Animals				Equipment Operators			
	Level I	Level II	Level III	Level IV	Level I	Level II	Level III	Level IV	Level I	Level II	Level III	Level IV
Balance of State (BOS) 1	$6.69	$7.69	$8.68	$9.68	$6.57	$7.31	$8.04	$8.78	$10.35	$11.25	$12.15	$13.05
Balance of State (BOS) 2	7.40	8.19	8.99	9.78	6.95	8.32	9.68	11.05	11.18	11.96	12.73	13.51
Balance of State (BOS) 3	7.70	8.97	10.24	11.51	6.61	7.20	7.80	8.39	9.71	11.06	12.40	13.75
Balance of State (BOS) 4	7.07	8.51	9.96	11.40	9.70	10.97	12.24	13.51	9.70	10.97	12.24	13.51
Bowling Green	N.A.	N.A.	N.A.	N.A.	6.58	7.81	9.04	10.27	10.28	10.78	11.29	11.79
Cincinnati-Middletown, Ohio-Kentucky-Indiana	8.23	9.32	10.41	11.50	7.79	9.66	11.52	13.39	9.13	10.28	11.43	12.58
Clarksville, Tennessee-Kentucky	6.64	7.97	9.29	10.62	6.64	7.72	8.79	9.87	9.34	10.24	11.13	12.03
Elizabethtown	7.30	7.98	8.67	9.35	7.01	8.29	9.57	10.85	10.28	10.78	11.27	11.77
Evansville, Indiana-Kentucky	6.28	7.55	8.82	10.09	10.38	11.25	12.11	12.98	10.13	11.00	11.87	12.74
Huntington-Ashland, West Virginia-Kentucky-Ohio	8.17	9.22	10.27	11.32	6.60	7.84	9.08	10.32	8.85	9.96	11.07	12.18
Lexington-Fayette	6.91	8.77	10.62	12.48	7.98	8.99	10.00	11.01	9.67	11.28	12.88	14.49

BLS area	Farmworkers and Laborers: Crop, Nursery, and Greenhouse				Farmworkers: Farm and Ranch Animals				Equipment Operators			
	Level I	Level II	Level III	Level IV	Level I	Level II	Level III	Level IV	Level I	Level II	Level III	Level IV
Louisville-Jefferson County, Kentucky-Indiana	7.05	7.90	8.74	9.59	7.71	8.99	10.26	11.54	9.91	10.71	11.52	12.32
Owensboro	6.26	7.28	8.31	9.33	6.57	7.51	8.45	9.39	10.32	11.09	11.85	12.62

Source: U.S. Department of Labor, Foreign Labor Certification Data Center, *Online Wage Library*, available at [http://www.flcdatacenter.com/OesWizardStart.aspx].

Note: As a reminder, the AEWR for Kentucky is $9.13 an hour (see table 1). Also, the proposed AEWR would be based on wage data from the OES survey, but it could not be less than $7.25 an hour.

Table 13. H-2A Prevailing Wages, North Carolina, 2008-2009

Area	Occupation	Prevailing Wage
Statewide		
	Cabbage, harvesting	$6.30 per hour
	Tomato, harvesting	$7.00 per hour
	Strawberry, harvesting	$7.00 per hour
	Cucumber, harvesting	$0.75 per 5/8 bushel
	Banana peppers, harvesting	No finding [a]
	Squash, harvesting	$6.50 per hour
	Grape, harvesting	$8.50 per hour
	Burley tobacco, harvesting	$9.00 per hour
	Watermelon, harvesting	$7.00 per hour
	Sweet corn, harvesting	$6.50 per hour
	Long green cucumber, harvesting	$0.50 per 5/8 bushel
	Jalapeno peppers, harvesting	$7.50 per hour
	Onion, harvesting	No finding
	Cantaloupe, harvesting	$6.40 per hour
	Pumpkin, harvesting	$8.00 per hour
	Sweet potato, harvesting	$0.40 per 5/8 bushel
Greenville		
	Tobacco, transplanting	$7.00 per hour
	Horticulture, cultivating	$6.90 per hour
	Tobacco, harvesting	$7.50 per hour
Mount Olive		
	Blueberry, harvesting	$5.00 per flat
	Tobacco, transplanting	$7.00 per hour
	Tobacco, harvesting	$7.00 per hour
	Horticulture, cultivating	$8.00 per hour
Raleigh		
	Tobacco, transplanting	$7.00 per hour
	Tobacco, harvesting	$7.00 per hour
	Horticulture, cultivating	$7.00 per hour

Area	Occupation	Prevailing Wage
Handersonville		
	Horticulture, cultivating	$8.00 per hour
	Christmas tree, harvesting	$8.00 per hour

Source: U.S. Department of Labor, Employment and Training Administration, Agricultural Online Wage Library, available at [http://www.foreignlaborcert.doleta.gov/aowl.cfm].

[a] "No finding" means that the number of workers in the sample for the occupation and area was too small to estimate a prevailing wage. (U.S. Department of Labor, Employment and Training Administration, Employment Service Forms Preparation Handbook, Handbook 385, August 1981, p. I-139.) When there is no finding from the prevailing wage survey, employers must pay at least the higher of the AEWR or the applicable minimum wage.

Table 14. H-2A Prevailing Wages, Georgia, 2008-2009

Area	Occupation	Prevailing Wage
Statewide		
	Yellow squash, pack	$6.00 per hour
North		
	Nursery, worker	$8.00 per hour
Central		
	Watermelon, cut	No finding a
	Watermelon, load	$80.00 per 22,000-pound bus
	Watermelon, packing shed	$7.00 per hour
	Watermelon, unload	$8.00 per hour
	Yellow squash, pick	No finding
	Yellow squash, pick	No finding
	Yellow squash, unload	No finding
	Yellow squash, pick, wash, grade and field pack	$1.00 per 6-gallon bucket
	Vidalia onions, pulling	$1.20 per 30 bundle bag, 100 plants
	Vidalia onions, pulling	$0.25 per 1 foot ply row
	Vidalia onions, field maintenance	$7.00 per hour
	Vidalia onions, driver	No finding
	Cabbage, driver	No finding
	Cabbage, cut and load	No finding
	Vidalia onions, planting	$0.0250 per foot 4 ply row
	Vidalia onions, clip and bag	$0.75 per 60-pound bag
	Vidalia onions, clip, bag/bucket and dump	$11.50 per bin (30 five-gallon buckets)
	Vidalia onions, driver	$7.00 per hour
	Vidalia onions, forklift driver	$7.50 per hour

Table 14. (Continued).

Area	Occupation	Prevailing Wage
	Vidalia onions, grader	$6.00 per hour
	Vidalia onions, load	$0.03 per 60-pound bag
	Vidalia onions, pack	$6.50 per hour
	Vidalia onions, unload	$0.03 per 60-pound bag
	Vidalia onions, bin setters	No finding
	Vidalia onions, box	No finding
	Vidalia onions, clip top, place on conveyor	No finding
	Vidalia onions, field maintenance	No finding
	Vidalia onions, experience forklift driver	No finding
	Vidalia onions, experience grader	No finding
	Vidalia onions, grader, experienced	No finding
	Vidalia onions, load flat bed	No finding
	Vidalia onions, load wagons	No finding
	Vidalia onions, load and unload	No finding
	Vidalia onions, machine operator	No finding
	Vidalia onions, sort	No finding
	Vidalia onions, unload with forklift	No finding
	Cucumber, pick, pack and grade	No finding
	Cucumber, grade	No finding
	Cucumber, pick	No finding
	Cucumber, truck driver	No finding
	Cucumber, pickles	No finding
	Cantaloupes, harvest	$0.06 per cantaloupe
	Cantaloupes, packing shed	No finding
	Nursery, worker	$7.00 per hour
	Grape tomatoes, truck driver	No finding
	Grape tomatoes, pick and palletize in	No finding
	Grape tomatoes, crew leader	No finding
	Grape tomatoes, bus driver	No finding
	Green tomato, pick, grade and field	No finding
	Green tomato, pick	No finding
	Green tomato, dumper	No finding
	Green tomato, driver, hauler	No finding
	Tomatoes, pick, grade, field box	No finding
	Tomatoes, pick	No finding
	Roma tomatoes, pick	No finding
	Watermelon, cut	$10.00 per hour
	Watermelon, cut and load	$120.00 per 18,000-pound trailer

Area	Occupation	Prevailing Wage
	Watermelon, cut and load	$80.00 per 13,000-pound trailer
	Watermelon, cut, load, unload, grade	No finding
	Watermelon, driver	$8.00 per hour
	Watermelon, load	$450.00 per 15,000-pound bus
	Watermelon, pack shed	$8.00 per hour
	Watermelon, tractor driver	No finding
	Watermelon, unload	$10.00 per hour
	Yellow squash, pick, wash, grade and	$6.00 per hour
	Yellow squash, pack	No finding
	Yellow squash, supervisor	No finding
	Zucchini, field supervisor	No finding
	Zucchini, pick, wash, grade and field	$6.00 per hour
	Corn, box maker	No finding
	Corn, checker	No finding
	Corn, crew leader	No finding
	Corn, field walker	No finding
	Corn, grade, pack and box at cooler	No finding
	Corn, lead row	No finding
	Corn, loader	No finding
	Corn, machine driver	No finding
	Corn, packer	No finding
	Corn, puller	No finding
	Corn, push down	No finding
	Corn, tie man	No finding
	Yellow squash, pick	No finding
	Zucchini, pick	No finding
	Cabbage, field cut	$0.26 per 50-pound box
	Cabbage, loading boxes	No finding
	Cabbage, pack on line	$5.50 per hour
	Cabbage, pick and field pack	$0.60 per 50-pound box
	Cabbage, unloading	No finding
	Greens, cut, bundle and box	$0.85 per 24 bunch box
	Greens, unloading	No finding
	Greens, cut and box	No finding
	Greens, icing	No finding
	Greens, loading	$0.10 per 1.35 bushel box
	Greens, packing shed	No finding
	Greens, unloading and icing	No finding
	Nursery, worker	$6.50 per hour
	Cucumber, dumper	No finding
	Cucumber, packing	$6.00 per hour

Table 14. (Continued).

Area	Occupation	Prevailing Wage
	Cucumber, picking	$0.35 per 5-gallon bucket
	Cucumber, pick, pack and grade	$8.51 per hour
	Cucumber, tractor driver	$8.00 per hour
	Cucumber, pack and dump	No finding
	Cucumber, pick, set bucket in trailer	No finding
	Cucumber, place and pack	No finding
	Bell pepper, pick	$6.00 per hour plus $0.10 per 5-gallon bucket
	Bell pepper, tractor driver	No finding
	Bell pepper, place and pack	No finding
	Bell pepper, pack	No finding
	Bell pepper, dumper	No finding
	Hot banana pepper, pick	No finding
	Peppers, pack	$6.75 per hour
	Peppers, pick	$0.30 per 7-gallon bucket
	Peppers, pick, grade and pack	$8.51 per hour
	Peppers, tractor driver	$8.00 per hour
	Peppers, box maker, stacker	No finding
	Peppers, dumper	No finding
	Peppers, grade	No finding
	Peppers, pick, set bucket in trailer	No finding
	Peppers, washers	No finding
	Eggplants, dumper	$6.67 per hour
	Eggplants, pack	$8.51 per hour
	Eggplants, pick	$0.50 per 7-gallon bucket
	Eggplants, pick, grade and pack	$8.51 per hour
	Eggplants, tractor driver	No finding
	Eggplants, box maker	No finding
	Eggplants, pick, pack and load	No finding
	Eggplants, stack	No finding
	Cantaloupes, harvest	$6.50 per hour
	Cantaloupes, packing shed	$6.00 per hour
	Cucumber, dumper	No finding
	Cucumber, packing	$6.00 per hour
	Cucumber, picking	$0.35 per 5-gallon bucket
	Cucumber, pick, pack and grade	$8.51 per hour
	Cucumber, tractor driver	$8.00 per hour
	Cucumber, pack and dump	No finding

Area	Occupation	Prevailing Wage
	Cucumber, pick, set bucket in trailer	No finding
	Cucumber, place and pack	No finding
	Bell pepper, pick	$6.00 per hour plus $0.10 per 5-gallon bucket
	Bell pepper, tractor driver	No finding
	Bell pepper, place and pack	No finding
	Bell pepper, pack	No finding
	Bell pepper, dumper	No finding
	Hot banana pepper, pick	No finding
	Peppers, pack	$6.75 per hour
	Peppers, pick	$0.30 per 7-gallon bucket
	Peppers, pick, grade and pack	$8.51 per hour
	Peppers, tractor driver	$8.00 per hour
	Peppers, box maker, stacker	No finding
	Peppers, dumper	No finding
	Peppers, grade	No finding
	Peppers, pick, set bucket in trailer	No finding
	Peppers, washers	No finding
	Eggplants, dumper	$6.67 per hour
	Eggplants, pack	$8.51 per hour
	Eggplants, pick	$0.50 per 7-gallon bucket
	Eggplants, pick, grade and pack	$8.51 per hour
	Eggplants, tractor driver	No finding
	Eggplants, box maker	No finding
	Eggplants, pick, pack and load	No finding
	Eggplants, stack	No finding
	Cantaloupes, harvest	$6.50 per hour
	Cantaloupes, packing shed	$6.00 per hour

Source: U.S. Department of Labor, Employment and Training Administration, *Agricultural Online Wage Library*, available at [http://www.foreignlaborcert.doleta.gov/aowl.cfm].

[a.] "No finding" means that the number of workers in the sample for the occupation and area was too small to estimate a prevailing wage. (U.S. Department of Labor, Employment and Training Administration, *Employment Service Forms Preparation Handbook*, Handbook 385, August 1981, p. I-139.) When there is no finding from the prevailing wage survey, employers must pay at least the higher of the AEWR or the applicable minimum wage.

Table 15. H-2A Prevailing Wages, Florida, 2008-2009

Area	Occupation	Prevailing Wage
Statewide		
	Corn, detassler- mechanical	No finding [a]
	Corn, cutter-puller	No finding
	Corn, packer-pusher	No finding
	Corn, crate maker	No finding
	Corn, crate stacker-loader	No finding
	Corn, crate closer-tie man	No finding
	Corn, ticket maker-checker	No finding
	Ticket writer operator-mobile packing	No finding
	Vegetable, assistant supervisor	No finding
	Blueberry, harvest	$4.00 per six-pound bucket
	Blueberry, packer	$7.00 per hour
	Blueberry, planter	No finding
	Citrus truck driver	$8.00 per hour
	Citrus fruit for processing, mechanical harvesting	No finding
	Early tangerine, hand harvest	$1.50 per 95-pound field box
	Late Tangerine, harvest, fresh market	$2.00 per field box
	Valencia orange, machine operator for processing	No finding
Central		
	Valencia oranges, harvest pickers for market	$0.90 per 90-pound field box plus end of season bonus
	Strawberry, planting	$10.00 per 1,000 plants
	Strawberry, harvest fresh market	$1.50 per 8 x 1 pound flat
	Early/mid orange harvest picker for processing	$0.85 per 90-pound field box
	Valencia orange, harvest for processing	$0.90 per 90-pound field box
	Grapefruit, hand harvest for fresh market	No finding
	Grapefruit, hand harvest for fresh market	$0.60 per field box
South		
	Agricultural equipment mechanic	$11.00 per hour
	Assistant supervisor, field operations	No finding
	Early/mid orange harvest picker for processing	$0.90 per 90-pound field box plus $0.01 to $0.03 per box end of season bonus
	Early/mid orange harvest picker for processing	$0.95 per 90-pound field box
	Early/mid orange, machine harvest for processing	No finding
	Valencia orange, harvest for processing	No finding

Area	Occupation	Prevailing Wage
	Grapefruit, hand harvest for processed fruit	No finding
	Grapefruit, hand harvest for fresh market	No finding
East Coast		
	Early/mid orange harvest picker for processing	$0.98 per 90-pound box

Source: U.S. Department of Labor, Employment and Training Administration, *Agricultural Online Wage Library*, available at [http://www.foreignlaborcert.doleta.gov/aowl.cfm].

[a]. "No finding" means that the number of workers in the sample for the occupation and area was too small to estimate a prevailing wage. (U.S. Department of Labor, Employment and Training Administration, *Employment Service Forms Preparation Handbook*, Handbook 385, August 1981, p. I-139.) When there is no finding from the prevailing wage survey, employers must pay at least the higher of the AEWR or the applicable minimum wage.

Table 16. H-2A Prevailing Wages, Kentucky, 2008-2009

Area	Occupation	Prevailing Wage
Statewide		
	Tobacco, cutting and housing	$8.00 per hour
	Tobacco, cutting	$8.00 per hour
	Tobacco, housing	$8.00 per hour
	Tobacco, stripping	$5.00 per hour

Source: U.S. Department of Labor, Employment and Training Administration, *Agricultural Online Wage Library*, available at [http://www.foreignlaborcert.doleta.gov/aowl.cfm].

REFERENCES

[1] According to the U.S. Department of Labor, final action on the proposed regulation is expected in November 2008. U.S. Department of Labor, Employment and Training Administration, *ETA Unified Agenda, Final Rule Stage*, available at [http://www.dol.gov/eta/regs/unifiedagenda/1205-AB55.htm].

[2] An H-2A worker is identified under 8 U.S.C. at 101(a)(15)(H)(ii)(a) of the Immigration and Nationality Act (INA) as a nonimmigrant alien seeking temporary employment in the United States.

[3] U.S. Department of Labor, Employment and Training Administration, *H-2A Certification for Temporary or Seasonal Agricultural Work*, available at

[http://www.foreignlaborcert.doleta.gov/h-2a.cfm]. (It is hereafter cited as Employment and Training Administration, *H-2A Certification for Temporary or Seasonal Agricultural Work*.)

[4] 20 CFR, § 655.102(b)(9). Employment and Training Administration, *H-2A Certification for Temporary or Seasonal Agricultural Work*.

[5] The number of H-2A visas issued in FY2007 is a preliminary count. For more information on the H-2A program, see CRS Report RL32044, *Immigration: Policy Considerations Related to Guest Worker Programs*, by Andorra Bruno.

[6] The number of H-2A visas issued is different from the number of workers certified by DOL. After DOL issues a labor certification, the employer petitions the U.S. Citizenship and Immigration Services (USCIS) to hire foreign workers. DOL's decision on the request for certification (whether approved or denied) is advisory to the USCIS. Also, an employer may hire fewer foreign workers than the number requested on the application for labor certification.

[7] The remaining certifications were for occupations such as cook, bee keeper, or fish hatchery worker (1.5%). The specific occupation for 13.0% of certifications could not be identified. The source for this information is our analysis of FY2007 H-2A labor certifications from the U.S. Department of Labor, "H-2A Program Data," *Foreign Labor Certification Online Wage Library and Data Center*, available at [http://www.flcdatacenter.com/CaseData.aspx].

[8] If workers are ranked from the lowest to the highest paid, workers at the 51st percentile earn more than 50% of workers; 49% of workers earn more than the wage at the 51st percentile. U.S. Department of Labor, Employment and Training Administration, *H-2A Program Handbook*, Handbook 398, January 1988, pp. II-1 to II-4. U.S. Department of Labor, Employment and Training Administration, *Employment Service Forms Preparation Handbook*, Handbook 385, August 1981, pp. I-111 to I-143.

[9] H-2A prevailing wage data are available, by state, at U.S. Department of Labor, Employment and Training Administration, *Agricultural Online Wage Library*, available at [http://www.foreignlaborcert.doleta.gov/aowl.cfm].

[10] For more information on the AEWR, see "Labor Certification Process for the Temporary Employment of Aliens in Agriculture in the United States: Adverse Effect Wage Rate Methodology," *Federal Register*, vol. 54, no. 127, July 5, 1989, pp. 28037-28051.

[11] For more information on the Farm Labor Survey, see U.S. Department of Agriculture, National Agriculture Statistics Service, "Farm Labor," *Surveys*, available at [http://www.nass.usda.gov/Surveys/Guide_to_NASS_Surveys/Farm_Labor/index.asp]. (It is hereafter cited as National Agriculture Statistics Service, "Farm Labor," *Surveys*.)

[12] Field workers are employees who plant, tend, and harvest crops. Livestock workers tend livestock, milk cows, and care for poultry. U.S. Department of Agriculture, National Agriculture Statistics Service, *Farm Labor*, February 15, 2008, available at [usda.mannlib.cornell.edu/usda/nass/FarmLabo/2000s/2008/FarmLabo-02-15-2008.pdf], p. 12. (It is hereafter cited as National Agriculture Statistics Service, *Farm Labor*, February 15, 2008.)

[13] U.S. Department of Agriculture, National Agriculture Statistics Service, *Agricultural Labor Survey Interviewer's Manual*, June 2005, pp. 104, 508-511. (It is hereafter cited as National Agriculture Statistics Service, *Agricultural Labor Survey Interviewer's Manual*.)

[14] National Agriculture Statistics Service, *Agricultural Labor Survey Interviewer's Manual*, p. 105. Annual averages are published in the November *Farm Labor* report.

[15] Service workers include contract laborers as well as harvesters who provide their own machinery, sheep shearers, milk testers, veterinarians, and others who provide services for a fee or under contract. National Agriculture Statistics Service, *Farm Labor*, February 15, 2008, p. 13.

[16] National Agriculture Statistics Service, "Farm Labor," *Surveys*.

[17] Since January 2003, the minimum wage in Alaska has been set at $7.15 an hour. State of Alaska, Division of Labor Standards and Safety, *Minimum Wage Standard and Overtime Hours*, available at [labor.state.ak.us/lss/whact.htm].

[18] Congress has also considered legislation to change the AEWR. For example, in the 110th Congress, the Agricultural Job Opportunities, Benefits, and Security Act of 2007 (the AgJOBS Act; S. 237, S. 340, and H.R. 371) would freeze the AEWR in each state at the rates in effect on January 1, 2003. The AEWR would be frozen at those rates for three years. At the end of the three-year period, the rates would be adjusted each March. The first adjustment would be the lesser of the annual change, beginning with 2006, in the CPI-U or 4%. Subsequent annual adjustments would be the lesser of the change in the CPI-U or 4%.

[19] U.S. Department of Labor, Employment and Training Administration, "Temporary Agricultural Employment of H-2A Aliens in the United States;

Modernizing the Labor Certification Process and Enforcement," *Federal Register*, vol. 73, February 13, 2008, pp. 8545, 8549-8552. (It is hereafter cited as Employment and Training Administration, *Temporary Agricultural Employment of H-2A Aliens in the United States; Modernizing the Labor Certification Process and Enforcement.*) The proposed rule would make several other changes to the H-2A program. For example, employers would no longer have to apply to DOL for a labor certification that qualified U.S. workers are not available and that the employment of foreign workers will not adversely affect the wages and working conditions of U.S. workers who are similarly employed. Instead, employers would have to "attest" to DOL that they have complied with all H-2A program requirements. Attestation is used in the H-1B professional speciality temporary worker program. For information on the H-1B program, see CRS Report RL30498, *Immigration: Legislative Issues on Nonimmigrant Professional Specialty (H-1B) Workers*, by Ruth Ellen Wasem.

[20] Published average hourly wages are based on information collected from the six most recent May and November survey samples. Wages from the first five samples are adjusted for inflation to produce average hourly wages in constant dollars. U.S. Department of Labor, Bureau of Labor Statistics, *Occupational Employment and Wages, 2006*, available at [stats.bls.gov/news.release/pdf/ocwage.pdf], Technical note.

[21] U.S. Department of Labor, Bureau of Labor Statistics, *Occupational Employment Statistics*, available at [http://www.bls.gov/OES]. U.S. Department of Labor, Bureau of Labor Statistics, *Occupational Employment and Wages, May 2005*, Bulletin 2585, available at [stats.bls.gov/oes/oes_pub_2005.htm], pp. 252-255. U.S. Census Bureau, *North American Industry Classification System (NAICS)*, available at [http://www.census.gov/epcd/www/naics.html], NAICS Code 11.

[22] An MSA consists of an urban center (or centers) and adjacent communities that have a high degree of economic and social integration. Executive Office of the President, Office of Management and Budget, *Metropolitan Statistical Areas, Metropolitan Divisions, Micropolitan Statistical Areas, Combined Statistical Areas, New England City and Town Areas, and Combined New England City and Town Areas*, OMB Bulletin No. 08-01, available at [http://www.whitehouse.gov/omb/bulletins/fy2008/b08-01.pdf], Appendix, p. 2. (It is hereafter cited at Office of Management and Budget, *Metropolitan Statistical Areas*.)

[23] Employment and Training Administration, *Temporary Agricultural Employment of H-2^a Aliens in the United States; Modernizing the Labor Certification Process and Enforcement*, p. 8574.

[24] U.S. Department of Labor, Employment and Training Administration, *Prevailing Wage Determination Policy Guidance, Non-Agricultural Immigration Programs*, May 9, 2005, available at [http://www.foreignlaborcert.doleta.gov/pdf/Policy_Nonag_Progs.pdf], p. 7. (It is hereafter cited as U.S. Department of Labor, *Prevailing Wage Determination Policy Guidance, Non-Agricultural Immigration Programs*.)

[25] To illustrate the four wage levels, assume that the Level I and Level IV hourly wage rates estimated from OES wage data are $10.00 and $22.00, respectively. The difference between the Level IV and Level I wage is $12.00. Dividing this difference by three and adding the result to the Level I wage yields a Level II wage of $14.00 (i.e., $12.00 ÷ 3 = $4.00. $10.00 + $4.00 = $14.00). Subtracting the result from the Level IV wage yields a Level III wage of $18.00 (i.e., $22.00 - $4.00 = $18.00).

[26] Detailed descriptions of these occupations are available at the U.S. Department of Labor, Bureau of Labor Statistics, *Farming, Fishing, and Forestry Occupations*, available at [http://www.bls.gov/soc/soc_r0a0.htm].

[27] Office of Management and Budget, *Metropolitan Statistical Areas*, p. 3.

[28] On May 25, 2007, President George W. Bush signed into law the U.S. Troop Readiness, Veterans' Care, Katrina Recovery, and Iraq Accountability Appropriations Act, 2007 (H.R. 2206, P.L. 110-28). Title VIII, Subtitle A, the Fair Minimum Wage Act of 2007, raised the basic federal minimum wage, in steps, from $5.15 to $7.25 an hour.

[29] U.S. Department of Labor, Employment Standards Administration, *Agricultural Employers Under the Fair Labor Standards Act (FLSA)*, available at [http://www.dol.gov/esa/whd/regs/compliance/whdfs12.pdf].

[30] The four OES wage levels are available by area and occupation at the U.S. Department of Labor, Foreign Labor Certification Data Center, *Online Wage Library*, available at [http://www.flcdatacenter.com/OesWizardStart.aspx].

[31] According to current rules, a wage determination that uses the four OES wage levels from the FLC Data Center begins with a Level I, or entry level, wage. For jobs that require greater skills or more experience, a higher wage applies. U.S. Department of Labor, *Prevailing Wage Determination Policy Guidance, Non-Agricultural Immigration Programs*, pp. 3, 7.

[32] U.S. workers include American citizens as well as foreign persons who have been legally admitted to the United States.

[33] According to the FLS, an estimated of 1,122,000 hired farmworkers were employed on U.S. farms and ranches during the week of October 7-13, 2007. Farmworkers include field and livestock workers employed directly by farmers and by agricultural service providers. U.S. Department of Agriculture, National Agriculture Statistics Service, *Farm Labor*, November 16, 2007, available at [usda.mannlib.cornell.edu/usda/nass/FarmLabo/2000s/2007/FarmLabo-11-16-2007.pdf], p. 1.

[34] U.S. Department of Labor, *Findings from the National Agricultural Workers Survey (NAWS) 2001-2002*, Research Report No. 9, March 2005, available at [http://www.doleta.gov/agworker/report9/naws_rpt9.pdf], p. 6.

[35] Wage estimates based on information collected from a sample of employers are subject to sampling error. Because the wage estimates from both the FLS and OES surveys are based on a sample of employers, a survey of all employers may yield different results.

[36] Employment and Training Administration, *Temporary Agricultural Employment of H-2^a Aliens in the United States; Modernizing the Labor Certification Process and Enforcement*, p. 8552.

In: Hired Farmworkers: Profile and Labor Issues   ISBN: 978-1-60741-232-8
Editor: Rea S. Berube, pp. 117-134   © 2009 Nova Science Publishers, Inc.

Chapter 3

FARM LABOR: THE ADVERSE EFFECT WAGE RATE (AEWR)*

William G. Whittaker

ABSTRACT

    American agricultural employers have long utilized foreign workers on a temporary basis, regarding them as an important labor resource. At the same time, the relatively low wages and acceptance of often difficult working conditions by such workers have caused them to be viewed as an economic threat to domestic American workers.

    To mitigate any "adverse effect" for the domestic workforce, a system of wage floors has been developed that applies, variously, both to alien and citizen workers — the *adverse effect wage rate* (AEWR). Under this system, a *guest worker* must be paid either the AEWR, the state or federal minimum wage, or the locally prevailing wage for his or her occupation, whichever is higher.

    An H-2A worker is identified under 8 U.S.C. at 101(a)(15)(H)(ii)(a) of the Immigration and Nationality Act as a nonimmigrant alien seeking temporary employment in the United States. Wages paid to H-2A and related workers are but one aspect of broader immigration questions. In this report, however, the issue is limited to domestic economic concerns. Use of guest workers has evolved from a relatively simple exchange of labor along the frontier between Mexico and the United States, responding to the

---

* Excerpted from CRS Report RL32861, dated March 26, 2008.

requirements of local employers, into a far more complicated structure that has expanded nationwide and involves many thousands of workers.

During World War I, Mexican workers were brought into the country to replace draftees. Later, during the Great Depression, those remaining in the States were subject to sporadic repatriation proceedings. During World War II, there was again perceived to be a need for guest workers; and, with the cessation of hostilities, there was also an effort to reduce the flow of aliens to the United States. Since the mid-1960s, several new programs involving guest workers have been instituted. In addition, numerous undocumented workers have entered (or re-entered) the country. Collectively, these guest workers, some have suggested, have come to compete with domestic (U.S.) workers — even where those domestic workers could be available for employment were conditions more favorable. Thus, the AEWR has been designed, in part, to deal with a putative surplus of alien workers but also to address any adverse impact upon domestic American workers.

This report is written from the perspective of labor policy, not of immigration policy. For discussion of immigration issues, see the Current Legislative Issues on the Congressional Research Service website [http://www.crs.gov].

American agricultural employers have long utilized foreign workers on a temporary basis, regarding them as an important labor resource. At the same time, the relatively low wages of such workers and their acceptance of often difficult working conditions have caused them to be viewed as an economic threat to American workers.

To mitigate any "adverse effect" for the domestic workforce, a system of wage floors has been developed that applies, variously, both to alien and to citizen workers. These systems have come to include (1) the *adverse effect wage rate* (AEWR), (2) both state and/or federal minimum wage rates, and (3) the locally prevailing wage rate — whichever is higher.

The AEWR deals specifically with agricultural workers (i.e., H-2A workers). It involves persons "having a residence in a foreign country *which he has no intention of abandoning*" and who are "coming temporarily to the United States to perform agricultural labor" of "a temporary or seasonal nature." (Italics added.) It is predicated upon the assumption that "... unemployed persons capable of performing such service or labor cannot be found" in the United States.[1] An AEWR has been developed for each state except Alaska (see table 1), and is announced early each year prior to the growing/production season.

INTRODUCTION

Where countries with widely different economies exist side-by-side, the more prosperous is likely to draw to itself workers from its lower-wage neighbors. Though wages of American agricultural workers are low in comparison with wage rates in the U.S. economy, they are relatively high by the standards of neighboring less developed countries. Thus, a continuing supply of workers has been available for employment in the United States at wage rates and under conditions that American workers, arguably, would not accept.

Low-wage labor has entered the United States from a variety of countries and under diverse circumstances. Indeed, importation of low-wage labor has been a long-standing tradition — with persons arriving in this country, moving into the fields and/or factories, gaining skills and becoming acclimated to American culture, and becoming citizens.[2] Here, our concern is largely with workers who have entered aspects of agricultural production: primarily citizens of Mexico but, as well, of several other countries.

Two migratory thrusts are at issue. On the one hand, there are workers who, attracted by relatively higher wages in the United States (or by other aspects of American society), have come to the States as immigrants seeking permanent employment and, normally, citizenship. Conversely, there has been a body of workers who, responding to U.S. public policy (and to the exigencies of the economy), have been encouraged to come north — not to seek citizenship but to provide employers with a continuing source of low-wage labor, and who, at the end of a work period, are expected to return to their country of origin. These latter individuals, speaking generally, are *guest workers*, and are affected by the AEWR.[3]

MEXICAN GUEST WORKER UTILIZATION: AN OVERVIEW

Through the past century, trends in immigration from Mexico north to the United States have reflected the motion of a pendulum. Sometimes, they have favored the Mexican worker; but, as often, they have favored employers and have had a mixed impact upon Mexicans and Americans.

In the late 19th and early 20th centuries, movement across the U.S.-Mexican frontier was relatively unrestricted. Mexican nationals joined a resident Mexican-American population in the fields and mines of the Southwest.[4] With World War I, workers from Mexico were recruited to offset the loss of American workers drafted into military service and were engaged for agricultural work, on the railways and in general industry as well.[5] After the war, a secondary problem arose: how to get the Mexican worker to go back to Mexico. This issue was aggravated by the Great Depression.[6] Then, World War II broke out and America turned once more to Mexico for low-skilled/low-wage labor. The result, in various forms, was the *bracero* program.[7]

By war's end, in 1945, agricultural employers had become accustomed to employing Mexican labor that was characterized at the time as docile, nonunion, temporary, and payable at low rates and, at the same time, as able and highly motivated. Through the process, a large body of Mexican workers had become acculturated to the American world of work. Having learned at least fragmentary English, they were able to function within the American system without the institutional support of the formal *bracero* program. In short, some might argue, the *bracero* program had been a training school for foreign workers operating outside the normal immigration structure. The *bracero*/guest worker programs, however, were also a source of contention, raising a number of socio-economic questions. Opposition continued to grow until, in 1964, the program was terminated.[8]

Even with termination, however, a body of foreign workers remained in the United States, augmented by Mexican workers who crossed the border without proper authorization.[9] These workers ("undocumented" or "illegal") may, it would seem, find themselves in competition with legal immigrants and native Americans for low-level work within agriculture and, increasingly, for other types of work as well. This raised several dilemmas. How might the demand of employers for low-wage labor be satisfied without imperiling the economic livelihood of resident/domestic American workers? And, as the ex-*bracero* community became a political force within the United States, how might these sometimes conflicting objectives be achieved without offending this new body of Americans?

COPING WITH "ADVERSE EFFECT"

Public concern over the impact of foreign workers has come to be addressed in immigration law. The Immigration and Nationality Act of 1952, as amended, provides for admission to the United States of a person (a) "having a residence in a foreign country which he has no intention of abandoning," (b) "who is coming temporarily to the United States to perform agricultural labor," (c) where the work is of "a temporary or seasonal nature," and (d) only "... if unemployed persons capable of performing such service or labor cannot be found in this country."[10] The act directs that a petition for admission of such persons (H-2A workers) "may not be approved by the Attorney General unless the petitioner [the prospective employer] has applied to the Secretary of Labor" for certification that

a   there are not sufficient workers who are able, willing, and qualified, and who will be available at the time and place needed, to perform the labor or services involved in the petition, and
b   the employment of the alien in such labor or services *will not* adversely affect the wages and working conditions of workers in the United States similarly employed.[11] (Italics added.)

If the requirements of paragraphs (A) and (B) are to be effective, they impose a heavy policy burden and responsibility upon the Secretary of Labor.[12]

Qualified and Willing

Paragraph (A) focuses upon the availability of workers. Are there domestic American workers who are "able" and "qualified" to satisfy the normally low or semi-skilled requirements of temporary agricultural labor? Did Congress mean to have the Secretary assess the skill and ability of each potential domestic agricultural laborer? If not, then these qualifications are reduced largely to a single standard: willingness to be employed. Even that measure can be complex. Must the potential worker be "willing" to work at whatever wage an employer may be willing to offer and under whatever conditions may exist — even if adverse?

Almost by definition, the H-2A worker is willing to accept a lower wage and conditions of labor generally more adverse than would be acceptable to most American workers. Thus (following documentable recruitment efforts), a prospective employer can affirm that American workers are unavailable and that the employer is only offering to the H-2A worker employment that American workers *do not want and will not accept*. In many other labor markets, movement toward higher wages and improved conditions could be expected to attract American workers.[13]

Will Not Affect Domestic Employment

As part of his responsibility under paragraph (A), the Secretary of Labor has developed a three-tiered wage rate requirement. The regulations state:

If the worker will be paid by the hour, the employer shall pay the worker at least the adverse effect wage rate in effect at the time the work is performed, the prevailing hourly wage rate, or the legal federal or State minimum wage rate, whichever is highest...[14]

The AEWR is set forth by the Department of Labor (DOL), based upon data gathered by the Department of Agriculture (DOA). DOA conducts a quarterly survey of the wages of field and livestock workers throughout the United States. The AEWR, then, is a weighted average of the DOA findings, calculated on a regional basis. It is adjusted, each year, taking into account prior experience with the change of the "average hourly wage rates for field and livestock workers (combined) based on the DOA Quarterly Wage Survey."[15] The rate (see table 1) is set for each state (except Alaska for which no rate has been fixed). The AEWR has no *direct* effect where an employer does not seek to engage H-2A workers. However, if he does engage H-2A workers and subsequently locates and hires American workers, then he is required to pay each group not less than the AEWR.

Paragraph (B) presents a more complex issue: demonstrating that employment of H-2A workers "will not adversely affect the wages and working conditions of workers in the United States similarly employed." Many view the AEWR structure as effectively setting a cap on the earnings of certain agricultural workers because agricultural employers may advertise for workers at the AEWR rate. If domestic workers are not available at the specified rate, the employer is allowed to employ foreign workers who, given the disparity in wage rates between Mexico and the United States, will almost always be available at the AEWR.

The H-2A option provides agricultural employers with an alternative source of labor and, in effect, expands the pool of available workers, potentially increasing competition for available jobs.[16] With that option open to them, agricultural employers may have no need to revise their recruitment and employment policies to make such employment more attractive to American workers.

Further, some may view the availability of foreign agricultural workers as a device through which to deter unionization among domestic agricultural workers. With the ready accessibility of foreign workers, there may be no need to bargain collectively with American workers over issues of wages and hours.[17]

Table 1. Adverse Effect Wage Rate by State, 1990-2008
(in current dollars per hour)

State[a]	1990	1991	1992	1993	1994	1995	1996	1997	1998	1999	2000	2001	2002	2003	2004	2005	2006	2007	2008
Alabama	4.29	4.46	4.91	5.04	5.43	5.66	5.40	5.92	6.30	6.30	6.72	6.83	7.28	7.49	7.88	8.07	8.37	8.51	8.53
Arizona	4.61	4.87	5.17	5.37	5.52	5.80	5.87	5.82	6.08	6.42	6.74	6.71	7.12	7.61	7.54	7.63	8.00	8.27	8.70
Arkansas	4.04	4.40	4.73	4.87	5.26	5.19	5.27	5.70	5.98	6.21	6.50	6.69	6.77	7.13	7.38	7.80	7.58	8.01	8.41
California	5.90	5.81	5.90	6.11	6.03	6.24	6.26	6.53	6.87	7.23	7.27	7.56	8.02	8.44	8.50	8.56	9.00	9.20	9.72
Colorado	4.51	5.00	5.29	5.44	5.57	5.62	5.64	6.09	6.39	6.73	7.04	7.43	7.62	8.07	8.36	8.93	8.37	8.64	9.42
Connecticut	4.98	5.21	5.61	5.82	5.97	6.21	6.36	6.71	6.84	7.18	7.68	8.17	7.94	8.53	9.01	9.05	9.16	9.50	9.70
Delaware	4.89	4.93	5.39	5.81	5.92	5.81	5.97	6.26	6.33	6.84	7.04	7.37	7.46	7.97	8.52	8.48	8.95	9.29	9.70
Florida	5.16	5.38	5.68	5.91	6.02	6.33	6.54	6.36	6.77	7.13	7.25	7.66	7.69	7.78	8.18	8.07	8.56	8.56	8.82
Georgia	4.29	4.46	4.91	5.04	5.43	5.66	5.40	5.92	6.30	6.30	6.72	6.83	7.28	7.49	7.88	8.07	8.37	8.51	8.53
Hawaii	7.70	7.85	7.95	8.11	8.36	8.73	8.60	8.62	8.83	8.97	9.38	9.05	9.25	9.42	9.60	9.75	9.99	10.32	10.86
Idaho	4.49	4.79	4.94	5.25	5.59	5.57	5.76	6.01	6.54	6.48	6.79	7.26	7.43	7.70	7.69	8.20	8.47	8.76	8.74
Illinois	4.88	5.05	5.59	5.85	6.02	6.18	6.23	6.66	7.18	7.53	7.62	8.09	8.38	8.65	9.00	9.20	9.21	9.88	9.90
Indiana	4.88	5.05	5.59	5.85	6.02	6.18	6.23	6.66	7.18	7.53	7.62	8.09	8.38	8.65	9.00	9.20	9.21	9.88	9.90
Iowa	5.03	4.85	5.15	5.65	5.76	5.72	5.90	6.22	6.86	7.17	7.76	7.84	8.33	8.91	9.28	8.95	9.49	9.95	10.44
Kansas	5.17	5.20	5.36	5.78	6.03	5.99	6.29	6.55	7.01	7.12	7.49	7.81	8.24	8.53	8.83	9.00	9.23	9.55	9.90
Kentucky	4.45	4.56	5.04	5.09	5.29	5.47	5.54	5.68	5.92	6.28	6.39	6.60	7.07	7.20	7.63	8.17	8.24	8.65	9.13
Louisiana	4.04	4.40	4.73	4.87	5.26	5.19	5.27	5.70	5.98	6.21	6.50	6.69	6.77	7.13	7.38	7.80	7.58	8.01	8.41
Maine	4.98	5.21	5.61	5.82	5.97	6.21	6.36	6.71	6.84	7.18	7.68	8.17	7.94	8.53	9.01	9.05	9.16	9.50	9.70

Table 1. (Continued).

State[a]	1990	1991	1992	1993	1994	1995	1996	1997	1998	1999	2000	2001	2002	2003	2004	2005	2006	2007	2008
Maryland	4.89	4.93	5.39	5.81	5.92	5.81	5.97	6.26	6.33	6.84	7.04	7.37	7.46	7.97	8.52	8.48	8.95	9.29	9.70
Massachusetts	4.98	5.21	5.61	5.82	5.97	6.21	6.36	6.71	6.84	7.18	7.68	8.17	7.94	8.53	9.01	9.05	9.16	9.50	9.70
Michigan	4.45	4.90	5.16	5.38	5.64	5.65	6.19	6.56	6.85	7.34	7.65	8.07	8.57	8.70	9.11	9.18	9.43	9.65	10.01
Minnesota	4.45	4.90	5.16	5.38	5.64	5.65	6.19	6.56	6.85	7.34	7.65	8.07	8.57	8.70	9.11	9.18	9.43	9.65	10.01
Mississippi	4.04	4.40	4.73	4.87	5.26	5.19	5.27	5.70	5.98	6.21	6.50	6.69	6.77	7.13	7.38	7.80	7.58	8.01	8.41
Missouri	5.03	4.85	5.15	5.85	5.76	5.72	5.90	6.22	6.86	7.17	7.76	7.84	8.33	8.91	9.28	8.95	9.49	9.95	10.44
Montana	4.49	4.79	4.94	5.25	5.59	5.57	5.76	6.01	6.54	6.48	6.79	7.26	7.43	7.70	7.69	8.20	8.47	8.76	8.74
Nebraska	5.17	5.20	5.36	5.78	6.03	5.99	6.29	6.55	7.01	7.12	7.49	7.81	8.24	8.53	8.83	9.00	9.23	9.55	9.90
Nevada	4.51	5.00	5.29	5.44	5.57	5.62	5.64	6.09	6.39	6.73	7.04	7.43	7.62	8.07	8.36	8.93	8.37	8.64	9.42
New Hampshire	4.98	5.21	5.61	5.82	5.97	6.21	6.36	6.71	6.84	7.18	7.68	8.17	7.94	8.53	9.01	9.05	9.16	9.50	9.70
New Jersey	4.89	4.93	5.39	5.81	5.92	5.81	5.97	6.26	6.33	6.84	7.04	7.37	7.46	7.97	8.52	8.48	8.95	9.29	9.70
New Mexico	4.61	4.87	5.17	5.37	5.52	5.80	5.87	5.82	6.08	6.42	6.74	6.71	7.12	7.61	7.54	7.63	8.00	8.27	8.70
New York	4.98	5.21	5.61	5.82	5.97	6.21	6.36	6.71	6.84	7.18	7.68	8.17	7.94	8.53	9.01	9.05	9.16	9.50	9.70
North Carolina	4.33	4.50	4.97	5.07	5.38	5.50	5.80	5.79	6.16	6.54	6.98	7.06	7.53	7.75	8.06	8.24	8.51	9.02	8.85
North Dakota	5.17	5.20	5.36	5.78	6.03	5.99	6.29	6.55	7.01	7.12	7/49	7.81	8.24	8.53	8.83	9.00	9.23	9.55	9.90
Ohio	4.88	5.05	5.59	5.85	6.02	6.18	6.23	6.66	7.18	7.53	7.62	8.09	8.38	8.65	9.00	9.20	9.21	9.88	9.90
Oklahoma	4.65	4.61	4.87	5.01	4.98	5.32	5.50	5.48	5.92	6.25	6.49	6.98	7.28	7.29	7.73	7.89	8.32	8.66	9.02
Oregon	5.42	5.69	5.94	6.31	6.51	6.41	6.82	6.87	7.08	7.34	7.64	8.14	8.60	8.71	8.73	9.03	9.01	9.77	9.94
Pennsylvania	4.89	4.93	5.39	5.81	5.92	5.81	5.97	6.26	6.33	6.84	7.04	7.37	7.46	7.97	8.52	8.48	8.95	9.29	9.70

State[a]	1990	1991	1992	1993	1994	1995	1996	1997	1998	1999	2000	2001	2002	2003	2004	2005	2006	2007	2008
Rhode Island	4.98	5.21	5.61	5.82	5.97	6.21	6.36	6.71	6.84	7.18	7.68	8.17	7.94	8.53	9.01	9.05	9.16	9.50	9.70
South Carolina	4.29	4.46	4.91	5.04	5.43	5.66	5.40	5.92	6.30	6.30	6.72	6.83	7.28	7.49	7.88	8.07	8.37	8.51	8.53
South Dakota	5.17	5.20	5.36	5.78	6.03	5.99	6.29	6.55	7.01	7.12	7.49	7.81	8.24	8.53	8.83	9.00	9.23	9.55	9.90
Tennessee	4.45	4.56	5.04	5.09	5.29	5.47	5.54	5.68	5.92	6.28	6.39	6.60	7.07	7.20	7.63	8.17	8.24	8.65	9.13
Texas	4.65	4.61	4.87	5.01	4.98	5.32	5.50	5.48	5.92	6.25	6.49	6.98	7.28	7.29	7.73	7.89	8.32	8.66	9.02
Utah	4.51	5.00	5.29	5.44	5.57	5.62	5.64	6.09	6.39	6.73	7.04	7.43	7.62	8.07	8.36	8.93	8.37	8.64	9.42
Vermont	4.98	5.21	5.61	5.82	5.97	6.21	6.36	6.71	6.84	7.18	7.68	8.17	7.94	8.53	9.01	9.05	9.16	9.50	9.70
Virginia	4.33	4.50	4.97	5.07	5.38	5.50	5.80	5.79	6.16	6.54	6.98	7.06	7.53	7.75	8.06	8.24	8.51	9.02	8.85
Washington	5.42	5.69	5.94	6.31	6.51	6.41	6.82	6.87	7.08	7.34	7.64	8.14	8.60	8.71	8.73	9.03	9.01	9.77	9.94
West Virginia	4.45	4.56	5.04	5.09	5.29	5.47	5.54	5.68	5.92	6.28	6.39	6.60	7.07	7.20	7.63	8.17	8.24	8.65	9.13
Wisconsin	4.45	4.90	5.16	5.38	5.64	5.65	6.19	6.56	6.85	7.34	7.65	8.07	8.57	8.70	9.11	9.18	9.43	9.65	10.01
Wyoming	4.49	4.79	4.94	5.25	5.59	5.57	5.76	6.01	6.54	6.48	6.79	7.26	7.43	7.70	7.69	8.20	8.47	8.76	8.74

Source: Compiled from data provided by the U.S. Department of Labor, Employment and Training Administration. See *Federal Register*, Feb. 26, 2003, pp. 8929-8930; Mar. 19, 2003, p. 13331; Mar. 3, 2004, pp. 10063-10065; Mar. 2, 2005, pp. 10152-10153; Mar. 16, 2006, pp. 13633-13635; Feb. 21, 2007, pp. 7909-7911; and Feb. 26, 2008, pp. 10288-10290.

[a] The U.S. Department of Agriculture (or of Labor) does not calculate an AEWR for Alaska.

STATE AND FEDERAL MINIMUM WAGE RATES

From an employee perspective, payment under the AEWR would seem to be preferred, given its relatively higher rate. But where the AEWR does not apply, other systems of compensation for H-2A and related domestic (or citizen) workers come into play: namely, the minimum wage, either the federal or the state minimum, whichever is higher, or the prevailing wage in the area.

For the several states and the federal government, the minima are statutory and set in a reasonably clear manner. However, establishment of the rate to be applied may be more complicated than would at first appear. In general, where there is an overlap, the higher standard (that most nearly in the interest of the worker) will normally prevail. But certain other qualifiers may need to be taken into account.

Not all workers are covered by the federal minimum wage, though most are. But where the states are concerned, there is a wide range of coverage and exemption. Some states, when setting their minima, have adopted what is, essentially, the federal system, moving higher as the local economy may suggest. Others supplement the federal system, dealing primarily with workers who would not be covered by federal rates. In states where tourism is heavy, states may have opted for coverage of tourist-related industries while largely ignoring workers in other industries. And some states have no state minimum wage structure at all. Most states, however, *do* have some individualized rates, and that may need to be taken into account. Again, however, one may want to recognize that coverage differs from one state to the next — and is often quite different.

Speaking generally, the federal minimum wage under the Fair Labor Standards Act (FLSA) is relatively stable. Although Congress is not required to revisit the act, it has done so at more or less regular intervals and will often project increases in the statutory rate through a series of steps, allowing employers an opportunity to plan for any changes that may occur. Each state, on the other hand, operates at its own initiative and, thus, changes may come at any time.

The AEWR is increased regularly each spring; and, while generally escalating, it presents a relatively consistent pattern of wages — though, again, one that is quite different from the state and federal minimum wage rates and from the locally prevailing wage. For a worker, the result may be confusing as he or she moves from one state to another and, perhaps, from the federal to a state minimum wage. Where the AEWR comes into play, workers both foreign and domestic (citizen or permanent resident workers) can count on a higher (and documentable) basis for payment.[18]

Still, certain generalizations can be made. As things currently stand, the lowest AEWR is now set at $8.41 per hour for certain jurisdictions in the South. The highest rate under the AEWR is $10.86 for Hawaii. The AEWR is higher than the minima (whether state or federal) in all cases. (table 2 demonstrates the extent to which the AEWR exceeds the state and federal minima.)

Were one to eliminate the AEWR and rely upon either the state or federal minimum wage rates, the result would be *a reduction* in the wages required to be paid to H-2A and related domestic (or citizen) workers. In some cases, the impact could be a substantial reduction in such earnings.

Table 2. Comparison of the Adverse Effect Wage Rate with State and Federal Minimum Wage Rates
(as of March 2008; in dollars)

State	Adverse Effect Wage Rate (AEWR)	State Minimum Wage Rate	Amount by Which the AEWR Exceeds the State Minimum	Federal Minimum Wage Rate	Amount by Which the AEWR Exceeds the Federal Minimum
Alabama	8.53	—	8.53	5.85	2.68
Arizona	8.70	6.90	1.80	5.85	2.85
Arkansas	8.41	6.25	2.16	5.85	2.56
California	9.72	8.00	1.72	5.85	3.87
Colorado	9.42	7.02	2.40	5.85	3.57
Connecticut	9.70	7.65	2.05	5.85	3.85
Delaware	9.70	7.15	2.55	5.85	3.85
Florida	8.82	6.79	2.03	5.85	2.97
Georgia	8.53	5.15	3.38	5.85	2.68
Hawaii	10.86	7.25	3.61	5.85	5.01
Idaho	8.74	5.85	2.89	5.85	2.89
Illinois	9.90	7.50	2.40	5.85	4.05
Indiana	9.90	5.85	4.05	5.85	4.05
Iowa	10.44	7.25	3.19	5.85	4.59
Kansas	9.90	2.65	7.25	5.85	4.05

Table 2. (Continued).

State	Adverse Effect Wage Rate (AEWR)	State Minimum Wage Rate	Amount by Which the AEWR Exceeds the State Minimum	Federal Minimum Wage Rate	Amount by Which the AEWR Exceeds the Federal Minimum
Kentucky	9.13	5.85	3.28	5.85	3.28
Louisiana	8.41	—	8.41	5.85	2.56
Maine	9.70	7.00	2.70	5.85	3.85
Maryland	9.70	6.15	3.55	5.85	3.85
Massachusetts	9.70	8.00	1.70	5.85	3.85
Michigan	10.01	7.15	2.86	5.85	4.16
Minnesota	10.01	6.15	3.86	5.85	4.16
Mississippi	8.41	—	8.41	5.85	2.56
Missouri	10.44	6.65	3.79	5.85	4.59
Montana	8.74	6.25	2.49	5.85	2.89
Nebraska	9.90	5.85	4.05	5.85	4.05
Nevada	9.42	6.33	3.09	5.85	3.57
New Hampshire	9.70	6.50	3.20	5.85	3.85
New Jersey	9.70	7.15	2.55	5.85	3.85
New Mexico	8.70	6.50	2.20	5.85	2.85
New York	9.70	7.15	2.55	5.85	3.85
North Carolina	8.85	6.15	2.70	5.85	3.00
North Dakota	9.90	5.85	4.05	5.85	4.05
Ohio	9.90	7.00	2.90	5.85	4.05
Oklahoma	9.02	5.85	3.17	5.85	3.17
Oregon	9.94	7.95	1.99	5.85	4.09
Pennsylvania	9.70	7.15	2.55	5.85	3.85

State	Adverse Effect Wage Rate (AEWR)	State Minimum Wage Rate	Amount by Which the AEWR Exceeds the State Minimum	Federal Minimum Wage Rate	Amount by Which the AEWR Exceeds the Federal Minimum
Rhode Island	9.70	7.40	2.30	5.85	3.85
South Carolina	8.53	—	8.53	5.85	2.68
South Dakota	9.90	5.85	4.05	5.85	4.05
Tennessee	9.13	—	9.13	5.85	3.28
Texas	9.02	5.85	3.17	5.85	3.17
Utah	9.42	5.85	3.57	5.85	3.57
Vermont	9.70	7.68	2.02	5.85	3.85
Virginia	8.85	5.85	3.00	5.85	3.00
Washington	9.94	8.07	1.87	5.85	4.09
West Virginia	9.13	6.55	2.58	5.85	3.28
Wisconsin	10.01	6.50	3.51	5.85	4.16
Wyoming	8.74	5.15	3.59	5.85	2.89

Source: *Federal Register*, vol. 73, no. 38, Feb. 26, 2008, pp. 10288-10290, and the U.S. Department of Labor, *Minimum Wage Laws in the States*, Jan. 1, 2008 [http://www.dol.gov/esa/]. Coverage may vary from one state to the next: reference will need to be made to each state's statute.

THE PREVAILING WAGE

As a standard for agricultural compensation, the prevailing wage may be somewhat more nebulous than either the AEWR or the minima, whether state or federal. It may be either higher or lower than either the AEWR or the applicable minimum rates. It may also be fraught with more complexities.

The prevailing wage applies to the individual task for which a worker has been hired, within the locality of the production process. In the manner of Davis-Bacon wage rate determinations (but applied, here, to agriculture), a prevailing rate will normally take into account local conditions: the nature and character of the crop, the fringe benefits an employer chooses to provide, any collateral responsibilities that may be a part of his or her job description or actual work. For activities in agriculture, there may need to be hundreds of individual prevailing wage rates.[19]

Some prevailing wage rates may already be available — where the prospective employer finds them more practical than the AEWR. Others may need to be calculated by either a state department of employment security or by the Department of Labor. The exigencies of the workplace may render such case-by-case judgments impractical; thus, it has also been suggested that, where an occupation is obscure (or at least not generally recognized within an area), an employer may need to develop his or her own standard so long as it is in keeping with generally accepted criteria.

An individual judgement by an employer may render a wage more consistent with local circumstances and allow a tailoring of compensation to the actual work to be performed. However, there may also be problems. The employee may very well be shut out of the process. Where work is of short duration, the employee may not be especially well acquainted with the circumstances of his or her employment. In addition, where there are language problems (with the worker only marginally literate in the language of the employer), bargaining may simply be set aside. In such cases, the market may establish the wage depending upon the urgency of need, either for employees or for the employer. Under such circumstances, there would seem to be an open invitation for misunderstanding, for an agency challenge, or for lawsuits, whether of a serious sort or frivolous.

It may be that the prevailing wage concept will not mesh neatly with the AEWR or the several minima.

REFERENCES

[1] 8 U.S.C. §§ 1 101(a)(15)(H)(ii)(a) and (b). See also CRS Report RL32044, *Immigration: Policy Considerations Related to Guest Worker Programs*, by Andorra Bruno.

[2] There is an extensive literature on the continuing quest of certain American employers for low-wage workers. See, for example, Roger Daniels, *Asian America: Chinese and Japanese in the United States Since 1850* (Seattle: University of Washington Press, 1988); Michael L. Conniff, *Black Labor on a White Canal: Panama, 1904-1981* (Pittsburgh: University

of Pittsburgh Press, 1984); and Edward D. Beechert, *Working in Hawaii: A Labor History* (Honolulu: University of Hawaii Press, 1985). For more recent experience, see Peter Kwong, *Forbidden Workers: Illegal Chinese Immigrants and American Labor*, (New York: The New Press, 1997); and Edna Bonacich and Richard P. Appelbaum, *Behind the Label: Inequality in the Los Angeles Apparel Industry* (Berkeley: University of California Press, 2000).

[3] U.S. agricultural workers can be divided into two groups: American workers and foreign workers. Herein, *American* workers are either U.S. citizens or permanent residents, and are distinguishable from *foreign* (alien, non-immigrant) workers who are in the country on a temporary basis. Further, some *foreign* workers may be here "legally" — others, "illegally."

[4] See, among other sources, Mark Reisler, *By The Sweat of Their Brow: Mexican Immigrant Labor in the United States, 1900-1940* (Westport: Greenwood Press, 1976); and Roberto R. Calderon, *Mexican Coal Mining Labor in Texas and Coahuila, 1880-1930* (College Station: Texas A & M University Press, 2000). On labor by native Americans, see portions of Evelyn Hu-DeHart, *Yaqui Resistance and Survival: The Struggle for Land and Autonomy, 1821-1910* (Madison: University of Wisconsin Press, 1984).

[5] Otey M. Scruggs, "The First Mexican Farm Labor Program," *Arizona and the West*, winter 1960, pp. 3 19-326.

[6] For the inter-war years and repatriation, see Abraham Hoffman, *Unwanted Mexican Americans in the Great Depression: Repatriation Pressures, 1929-1939* (Tucson: University of Arizona Press, 1979 edition); and Francisco E. Balderrama and Raymond Rodriguez, *Decade of Betrayal: Mexican Repatriation in the 1930s* (Albuquerque: University of New Mexico Press, 1995).

[7] Concerning the bracero program during World War II and its implications, see Otey M. Scruggs, *Braceros, "Wetbacks," and the Farm Labor Problem: Mexican Agricultural Labor in the United States, 1942-1954* (New York: Garland Publishing, 1988); and Richard B. Craig, *The Bracero Program: Interest Groups and Foreign Policy* (Austin: University of Texas Press, 1971).

[8] See Craig, *op. cit.*, and Ellis W. Hawley, "The Politics of the Mexican Labor Issue, 1950- 1965," *Agricultural History*, July 1966, pp.1 57-176.

[9] Stephen H. Sosnick, in *Hired Hands: Seasonal Farm Workers in the United States* (Santa Barbara: McNally & Loftin, West, 1978, p. 9), noted that during its

peak year (1957), some "450,000 braceros did seasonal farm work in the United States. Since the bracero program ended, their place has been taken by about 30,000 legal commuters from Mexico and by a large number — perhaps 200,000 — of illegal commuters and illegal residents, *many of whom are former braceros.*" (Italics added.)

[10] 8 U.S.C. §§ 1101(a)(15)(H)(ii)(a) and (b).

[11] 8 U.S.C. §§ 1 188(a)(1)(A) and (B).

[12] The conditions under which H-2A workers may be employed are set forth in detail in 20 C.F.R. Part 655. The AEWR is only one small aspect of the H-2A program. For a discussion of the program and of current issues, see CRS Report RL30852, *Immigration of Agricultural Guest Workers: Policy, Trends, and Legislative Issues*, by Ruth Wasem and Geoffrey Collver (out of print but available upon request from the author). See, also, Howard N. Dillon, "Foreign Agricultural Workers and the Prevention of Adverse Effect," *Labor Law Journal*, December 1966, pp. 739-748.

[13] Sosnick, *op. cit.*, p. 387, states: "For most types of work done in the United States, the only way employers can overcome a shortage of job-seekers is to make the jobs more attractive. For seasonal farm work, however, employers are permitted to bring in workers from foreign countries." Questions persist about possible farm labor shortages and the impact of foreign workers on wages and the local community. See CRS Report RL30395, *Farm Labor Shortages and Immigration Policy*, by Linda Levine. Through recent years, non-agricultural firms have followed agriculture's initiative and pressed for more guest workers, banding together as the 'Essential Worker Immigration Coalition' (EWIC). See "Essential Worker Immigration Coalition Resumes Lobbying," National Journal's *Congress Daily*, March 15, 2002; and the Bureau of National Affairs, *Daily Labor Report*, July 28, 2003, p. A6. See, also, the EWIC website at [http://www.ewic.org].

[14] 20 C.F.R. § 655.1 02(b)(9)(i). The regulations set out separate requirements if the worker is paid on a piece rate basis. See 20 C.F.R. § 655.102(b)(9)(ii).

[15] 20 C.F.R. § 655.207(a), (b) and (c). Concerning the methodology for calculation of the AEWR, see *Federal Register*, June 1, 1987, pp. 20496-20533, and *Federal Register*, July 5, 1989, pp. 28037-2805 1.

[16] "There seems to be only one practicable way to slow the influx of illegal aliens," states Sosnick, *op. cit.*, p. 440, and that is "... to make it difficult for them to obtain employment in the United States." This assumes that it

is public policy for "the influx of illegal aliens" to be slowed. See discussion of "criteria orders" on pp. 404-405.

[17] There has been, through the years, some concern that *guest workers* might be used to break strikes or, otherwise, to be involved in labor disputes. In 1974, Guinn Sinclair, president, National Farm Labor Contractors Association, pointed to an almost "complete lack of legislation" on what "constitutes a labor dispute" in the agricultural sector. "Does a labor dispute exist when the United Farm Workers Union issues a boycott of lettuce and table grapes?" See U.S. Congress, Senate, Subcommittee on Employment, Poverty, and Migratory Labor, Committee on Labor and Public Welfare, *Farm Labor Contractor Registration Act Amendments, 1974,* Fresno, Cal., February 8, 1974, and Washington, D. C., April 9, 1974, pp. 32-33. The Farm Bureau raised similar objections: "...what constitutes a strike, slowdown or labor-management dispute" and when does "such a condition exist at a particular farm." See *ibid,* p. 163.

[18] In 2007 (H.R. 2206), Congress raised the federal minimum wage in steps as follows: to $5.85 per hour as of July 24, 2007; to $6.55 per hour as of July 24, 2008; and to $7.25 per hour after July 24, 2009. Several of the states have adopted the concept of indexation where the state minima are concerned, raising the rate automatically on the basis of systems of economic variables.

[19] The Davis-Bacon Act requires that not less than the locally prevailing wage be paid to workers engaged *in construction* to which the federal government is a party. It does not apply to agricultural workers and is used, here, only as an example of the complexities of calculation. In 1998, Carlotta Joyner, Director, Education and Employment Issues, General Accountability Office, observed that in surveying construction wage rates for Davis-Bacon purposes, DOL was required to survey some "3,000 individual counties or groups of counties ... for four different types of construction." Then, within each type, there were diverse construction crafts to be surveyed. Setting a locally prevailing wage for employment in agriculture could be as complex. See testimony of Joyner before the Subcommittee on Labor, Health and Human Services, and Education, Committee on Appropriations, February 5, 1998, p. 13 of her prepared text (GAO/T-HEHS-98-88). See also CRS Report 94-408, *The Davis-Bacon Act: Institutional Evolution and Public Policy,* by William G. Whittaker.

In: Hired Farmworkers: Profile and Labor Issues   ISBN: 978-1-60741-232-8
Editor: Rea S. Berube, pp. 135-159   © 2009 Nova Science Publishers, Inc.

Chapter 4

FARM LABOR SHORTAGES AND IMMIGRATION POLICY[*]

Linda Levine

ABSTRACT

The connection between farm labor and immigration policies is a longstanding one, particularly with regard to U.S. employers' use of workers from Mexico. The Congress is revisiting the issue as it debates guest worker programs, increased border enforcement, and employer sanctions to curb the flow of unauthorized workers. Two decades ago, the Congress passed the Immigration Reform and Control Act (IRCA, P.L. 99-603) to reduce illegal entry into the United States by imposing sanctions on employers who knowingly hire persons who lack permission to work in the country. In addition to a general legalization program, IRCA included legalization programs specific to the agricultural industry that were intended to compensate for the act's expected impact on the farm labor supply and encourage development of a legal crop workforce. These provisions of the act have not operated in the offsetting manner that was intended: substantial numbers of unauthorized aliens have continued to join legal farm workers in performing seasonal agricultural services (SAS).

A little more than one-half of the SAS workforce is not authorized to hold U.S. jobs. Crop growers contend that their sizable presence implies a shortage of native- born farm workers. Grower advocates argue that farmers would rather not employ unauthorized workers because doing so puts them at risk of incurring penalties. Farm worker advocates counter that crop

---

[*] Excerpted from CRS Report RL30395, dated January 17, 2008.

growers prefer unauthorized workers because they are in a weak bargaining position. If the supply of unauthorized workers were curtailed, it is claimed, farmers could adjust to a smaller workforce by introducing labor-efficient technologies and management practices, and by raising wages, which, in turn, would entice more U.S. workers to accept farm jobs. Growers respond that further mechanization would be difficult for some crops, and that much higher wages would make the U.S. industry uncompetitive in world markets without expanding the legal farm workforce. These remain untested arguments because perishable crop growers have rarely, if ever, operated without unauthorized foreign-born workers.

Trends in the agricultural labor market generally do not suggest the existence of a nationwide shortage of domestically available farm workers, in part because the government's databases cover authorized and unauthorized workers. While nonfarm employment generally has increased thus far in the current decade, farm jobs generally have decreased. The length of time hired farm workers are employed has changed little or fallen over the years as well. Their unemployment rate has varied slightly and remains well above the U.S. average. Underemployment among farm workers also remains substantial. In addition, the earnings of farm workers relative to other private sector employees has changed little over time.

This assessment does not preclude the possibility of labor shortages in particular geographic areas at particular times of the year. Some statistical evidence suggests that California growers experienced a tighter labor market in July 2007 compared to peak harvest season a year earlier. It nonetheless appears that the offer of larger wage increases than those of employers in other industries contributed to there being sufficient (authorized and unauthorized) workers available to enable California growers to increase employment on their farms in the year ended July 2007.

INTRODUCTION

Questions often have arisen over the years about (1) whether sufficient workers are available domestically to meet the seasonal employment demand of perishable crop producers in the U.S. agricultural industry[1] and (2) how, if at all, the Congress should change immigration policy with respect to farm workers. Immigration policy has long been intertwined with the labor needs of crop (e.g., fruit and vegetable) growers, who rely more than most farmers on hand labor (e.g., for harvesting) and consequently "are the largest users of hired and contract workers on a per-farm basis."[2] Since World War I, the Congress has allowed the use of temporary foreign workers to perform agricultural labor of a seasonal nature as a means of augmenting the supply of domestic farm workers.[3] In addition, a sizeable fraction of immigrants historically have found employment on the nation's farms.[4]

The intersection between farm labor and immigration has again emerged as a policy issue. The terrorist attacks of September 11, 2001 effectively quashed the discussions on this subject between the Bush and Fox Administrations that took place shortly after President Bush first came into office, but the proposal of a broad-based temporary foreign worker program that President Bush sketched in December 2003 revived interest in the labor-immigration nexus. (For a discussion of bills and the President's proposal, see CRS Report RL32044, *Immigration: Policy Considerations Related to Guest Worker Programs*, by Andorra Bruno.) The lack of progress on broad-based immigration reform before the summer 2007 recess has led to speculation that Congress now will narrow its focus to the supply of temporary foreign workers to the agricultural sector and to professional specialty occupations.

This report first explains the connection made over the past several years between farm labor and immigration policies. It next examines the composition of the seasonal agricultural labor force and presents the arguments of grower and farm worker advocates concerning its adequacy relative to employer demand. The report then analyzes trends in employment, unemployment, time worked and wages of authorized and unauthorized farm workers to determine whether they are consistent with the existence of a nationwide shortage of domestically available farm workers. The farm labor supply-demand situation by geographic area is examined as well.

FARM WORKERS AND ACTIVITIES OF SSA AND DHS

During the second half of the 1990s, attention began to focus on the growing share of the domestic supply of farm workers that is composed of aliens who are not authorized to work in the United States. The U.S. Department of Labor (DOL) estimated that foreign-born persons in the country illegally accounted for 37% of the domestic crop workforce in FY1 994-FY1 995. Shortly thereafter (FY1 997-FY1 998), unauthorized aliens' share of the estimated 1.8 million workers employed on crop farms reached 52%.[5] By FY1999-FY2000, their proportion had increased to 55% before retreating somewhat — to 53% — in FY2001-FY2002.[6]

Although a number of studies found that no nationwide shortage of domestic farm labor existed in the past decade,[7] a case has been made that the considerable presence of unauthorized foreign-born workers in seasonal agriculture implies a lack of legal workers relative to employer demand. Arguably, the purported imbalance between authorized-to-work farm labor and employer demand would become more apparent were the supply of unauthorized workers curtailed sufficiently — a fear that has plagued growers for some time.

Crop producers and their advocates have testified at congressional hearings and asserted in other venues that they believe the latest risk of losing much of their labor force comes from efforts by the Bureau of Citizenship and Immigration Services and the Bureau of Immigration and Customs Enforcement within the Department of Homeland Security (DHS) to step-up employment verification and enforcement activities, in concert with mailings of no-match letters by the Social Security Administration (SSA). Growers have asserted that these activities disrupt their workforces by increasing employee turnover and therefore, decreasing the stability of their labor supply. The perception that government actions negatively affect U.S. agriculture has prompted a legislative response in the past.

COMPOSITION OF THE SEASONAL FARM LABOR FORCE

Immigration legislation sometimes has been crafted to take into account the purported labor requirements of U.S. crop growers. In 1986, for example, Congress passed the Immigration Reform and Control Act (IRCA, P.L. 99-603) to curb the presence of unauthorized aliens in the United States by imposing sanctions on employers who knowingly hire individuals who lack permission to work in the country. In addition to a general legalization program, P.L. 99-603 included two industry-specific legalization programs — the Special Agricultural Worker (SAW) program and the Replenishment Agricultural Worker (RAW) program[8] — that were intended to compensate for the act's expected impact on the farm labor supply and encourage the development of a legal crop workforce. These provisions of the act have not operated in the offsetting manner that was intended, however, as substantial numbers of unauthorized aliens have continued to join legal farm workers in performing seasonal agricultural services (SAS).[9]

On the basis of case studies that it sponsored, the Commission on Agricultural Workers concluded in its 1992 report that individuals legalized under the SAW program and other farm workers planned to remain in the agricultural labor force "indefinitely, or for as long as they are physically able."[10] According to the DOL's National Agricultural Workers Survey, two-thirds of so-called SAWs stated that they intended to engage in field work until the end of their working lives.[11]

For many SAWs, the end of their worklives — at least their worklives in farming — may now be near at hand. The diminished physical ability generally associated with aging in combination with the taxing nature of crop tasks could well be prompting greater numbers of SAWs to leave the fields. Relatively few farm workers are involved in crop production beyond the age of 44 and even fewer beyond the age of 54 (19% and 7%, respectively, in FY2001-FY2002).[12] The Commission on Agricultural Workers noted that the typical SAW in 1990 was a 30-year-old male who "is likely to remain in farm work well into the 21st century."[13] As the "average age of SAW-legalized workers in 2007 will be 47," increasing numbers of them are likely to be curtailing their participation in SAS labor force.[14] It thus appears that the 1986 legalization program has become less useful over time in fulfilling the labor requirements of crop producers.

A combination of factors likely has contributed to the decrease in SAWs' share of agricultural employment.[15] While the share of IRCA-legalized farm workers has been falling over time due to aging and the availability of nonfarm jobs, the leading factor probably is the substantially increased presence of illegal aliens.[16] In the first half of the 1990s, unauthorized workers rose from 7% to 37% of the SAS labor force.[17] Their share climbed to 52% by FY1997-FY1998;[18] then, rose further to 55% by FY1999-FY2000, before it dropped somewhat to 53% in FY2001-FY2002.[19] Moreover, the number of SAS workdays performed by unauthorized aliens more than tripled between FY1989 and FY2002.[20] In addition, of the many foreign-born newcomers to the sector in FY2000-FY2002, 99% were employed without authorization.

Unauthorized aliens, arguably, have been displacing legal workers from jobs in the agricultural industry. Farm worker advocates assert that crop producers prefer unauthorized employees because they have less bargaining power with regard to wages and working conditions than other employees. Growers counter that they would rather not employ unauthorized workers because doing so puts them at risk of incurring penalties. They argue that the considerable presence of unauthorized aliens in the U.S. farm labor force implies a shortage of legal workers.

Farm worker groups and some policy analysts contend that even if the previously mentioned DHS and SSA activities were to deprive farmers of many of their unauthorized workers, the industry could adjust to a smaller supply of legal workers by (1) introducing labor-efficient technologies and management practices, and (2) raising wages which, in turn, would entice more authorized workers into the farm labor force. Grower advocates respond that further mechanization would be difficult to develop for many crops and that, even at higher wages, not many U.S. workers would want to perform physically demanding, seasonal farm labor under variable climactic conditions. Moreover, employer representatives and some policy analysts maintain that growers cannot raise wages substantially without making the U.S. industry uncompetitive in world markets which, in turn, would reduce farm employment. In response, farm worker supporters note that wages are a small part of the price consumers pay for fresh fruits and vegetables and accordingly, higher wages would result in only a slight rise in retail prices. These remain untested arguments as perishable crop growers have rarely, if ever, had to operate without unauthorized aliens in their workforces.

A Farm Labor Shortage?

Trends in the farm labor market generally do not suggest the existence of a nationwide shortage of domestically available farm workers, in part because the government's statistical series cover authorized and unauthorized workers. This overall finding does not preclude the possibility of spot shortages of farm labor in certain areas of the country at various times of the year.

Caution should be exercised when reviewing the statistics on farm workers' employment, unemployment, time worked and wages that follow. The surveys from which the data are derived cover somewhat different groups within the farm labor force (e.g., all hired farm workers as opposed to those engaged only in crop production or workers employed directly by growers as opposed to those supplied to growers by farm labor contractors), and they have different sample sizes. A household survey such as the Current Population Survey (CPS) could well understate the presence of farm workers because they are more likely to live in less traditional quarters (e.g., labor camps) and of unauthorized workers generally because they may be reluctant to respond to government enumerators. And, some of the surveys have individuals as respondents (e.g., the CPS and DOL's National Agricultural Workers Survey) while others have employers as respondents (e.g., the U.S. Department of Agriculture's National Agricultural Statistics Service Farm Labor Survey, FLS). Surveys that query employers are more likely to pickup unauthorized employment than are surveys that query individuals.

Underlying Assumptions

Estimating whether the number of workers in the United States is sufficient to fulfill employer demand is difficult because there is no agreed-upon definition of a labor shortage. Economists believe labor markets reach a balance between supply and demand, with a lag, absent government policies that prevent a shortage or surplus from occurring. For example, economic theory posits that firms needing more workers to fill jobs in a particular occupation will initially raise wages to attract employees from elsewhere in the economy and thereby restore equilibrium between supply and demand in the occupation. In contrast, businesses tend to think there is a shortage in a given occupation if as many workers as they want cannot be obtained at the current wage being offered.

Estimating shortages or surpluses also is not straight-forward because the supply of and demand for labor generally cannot be measured directly. There is no proxy for the supply of workers to most occupations.[21] An oft-used measure of demand is employment. Accordingly:

- an increase in an occupation's employment denotes that employers have increased their demand for labor and may be moving toward — but have not reached — a shortfall of workers, while
- a decrease in an occupation's employment signals that employers either have

1 reduced their demand for labor and may be moving away from a shortage, or
2 maintained or increased their demand but may have exhausted the supply of readily available workers.

The trend in wages commonly is used to clarify the latter situation: if employment in an occupation falls despite employers substantially bidding up wages, it is assumed that the number of workers readily available to fill jobs in the occupation may have reached its limit.

Other measures that can be examined to shed additional light on the relationship between labor supply and demand include unemployment and time worked. Both these indicators are analyzed below to supplement trends in farm employment and wages.

Employment

Although the employment of hired workers engaged in crop or livestock production (including contract workers) has fluctuated erratically over time, the trend overall has been downward (see columns 3 and 7 in table 1). The employment pattern among crop workers hired directly by growers (i.e., excluding those supplied by farm labor contractors and crew leaders) has regularly risen and then fallen back, but to a higher level through 2000 (column 4). This ratcheting upward of employment produced a 12% gain over the 1990-2000 period. In contrast, other wage and salary workers experienced steady and robust job growth over almost the entire period: from 1990 to 2000, wage and salary employment in nonfarm industries advanced by 18%. These divergent employment patterns suggest that hired farm workers did not share equally in the nation's long economic expansion and appear to be inconsistent with the presence of a nationwide farm labor shortage at that time.

The labor market continued to contract in 2002, despite the 2001 recession's end in November 2001. Nonfarm wage and salary employment showed signs of revival in 2003 that have since continued. In contrast, employment of hired farm workers has not followed a consistently upward trend. (See columns 3 and 7 of table 1).

Table 1. Hired Farm Employment (numbers in thousands)

Year	Total Nonfarm Wage & Salary Employment[a]	Economic Research Service (ERS)[b]		National Agricultural Statistics Service (NASS)[c]		
		Hired Farm Workers[d]	Hired Crop Workers[e]	Hired Farm Workers[f]	Agricultural Service Workers[g]	Total
1990	105,705	886	419	892	250	1,142
1991	104,520	884	449	910	259	1,169
1992	105,540	848	409	866	252	1,118
1993	107,011	803	436	857	256	1,113
1994	110,517	793	411	840	250	1,090
1995	112,448	849	433	869	251	1,120
1996	114,171	906	451	832	236	1,068
1997	116,983	889	432	876	240	1,116
1998	119,019	875	458	880	246	1,126
1999	121,323	840	440	929	233	1,162
2000	125,114	878	468	890	243	1,133
Year	Total Nonfarm Wage & Salary Employment[a]	Economic Research Service (ERS)[b]		National Agricultural Statistics Service (NASS)[c]		
		Hired Farm Workers[d]	Hired Crop Workers[e]	Hired Farm Workers[f]	Agricultural Service Workers[g]	Total
2001	125,407	745	392	881	244	1,125
2002	125,156	793	370	886	225	1,111
2003	126,015	777	372	836	236	1,072

2004	127,463	712	368	825	277	1,102
2005	129,931	730	393	780	282	1,062
2006	132,449	748	351	752	255	1,007

Source: Created by the Congressional Research Service (CRS) from sources cited below.

[a] Data are from the monthly CPS, a survey of households, as reported by the DOL's Bureau of Labor Statistics (BLS) for individuals age 16 or older.

[b] Data are from the monthly CPS as reported by the U.S. Department of Agriculture's ERS for individuals age 15 or older.

[c] Data are from the Farm Labor Survey (FLS), a quarterly survey of farm operators, as reported by the U.S. Department of Agriculture's NASS. The statistics reflect individuals on employers' payrolls during the survey week in January, April, July, and October. Data for Alaska are not included.

[d] In the CPS, an individual's occupation is based on the activity in which he spent the most hours during the survey week. Hired farm workers are those whose primary job is farm work and for which they receive wages, as opposed to unpaid family workers or self-employed farmers. Hired farm workers include individuals engaged in planting, cultivating, and harvesting crops or tending livestock whom growers employ directly or through agricultural service providers (e.g., farm labor contractors and crew leaders), as well as farm managers, supervisors of farm workers, and nursery and other workers.

[e] The ERS disaggregates hired farm workers by the kind of establishment employing them (i.e., establishments primarily engaged in crop production, livestock production or other). As "other" includes agricultural service providers, the figures for crop workers are limited to farm workers whom growers employ directly.

[f] Persons paid directly by farmers, including field workers (i.e., those who plant, cultivate and harvest crops), livestock workers (i.e., those who tend livestock, milk cows or care for poultry), supervisory workers (e.g., managers or range foremen), and other workers on farmers' payrolls (e.g., bookkeepers, secretaries or pilots).

[g] Persons supplied to farmers to perform harvest work, for example, but paid by agricultural service firms (e.g., farm labor contractors or crew leaders). Agricultural service workers perform work on farms on a contract or fee basis (e.g., veterinarian services, sheep shearing).

July Farm Employment by State

Farm employment is subject to considerable seasonal variation which annual average data masks. Demand for hired farm labor typically peaks in July when many crops are ready to be harvested. The July employment statistics from the FLS have ranged from less than 1.1 million to less than 1.5 million since 1990, well above the average for some years shown in the last column of table 1. Farm employment also varies greatly by geographic area. Recent July data disaggregated by geographic area available from the FLS are examined below to assess whether demand at its peak has produced labor shortages in some parts of the country.

Employment of hired workers and agricultural service workers rose 0.8% on the nation's farms between July 2006 and July 2007, while in Florida total farm employment fell. (See table 2.) When compared with the 1.0% increase in employment among nonfarm wage and salary workers in 2007, the FLS data do not suggest that peak demand for farm workers nationwide and in Florida exceeded the domestically available supply of labor this past July.[22]

Table 2. Total Farm Employment in the United States (excluding Alaska) and in California and Florida, July 2005-July 2007

July	Hired Farm Workers and Agricultural Service Workers Working on Farms					
	Number (in thousands)			Percent Change		
	United States	Florida	California	United States	Florida	California
2005	1344	43	347			
2006	1196	46	302	-11.0	6.9	-12.9
2007	1205	43	322	0.8	-6.5	6.6

Source: U.S. Department of Agriculture, National Agricultural Statistics Service, *Farm Labor*, August releases.

Note: See footnotes in table 1 for definitions of hired farm worker and agricultural service worker.

The situation differed considerably for California growers. Total farm employment in the state rose at an above-average rate of 6.6% as shown in table 2. The large job growth rate suggests California's farmers faced a comparatively tight labor market this past July.

The state's high rate of job growth on farms largely was due to greater use of workers supplied by farm labor contractors. As shown in table 3, employment of hired farm workers in California increased by 0.5% (1,000) between July 2006 and July 2007. Over the same period, employment of agricultural service workers increased by 17.1% or 19,000 (from 111,000 to 130,000) according to data from the FLS. California's greater use of agricultural service workers accounted for one-half of the increase in employment of these workers at the national level (38,000).

Table 3. Number of Hired Farm Workers by Geographic Area, July 2005-July 2007

Area	Number of Hired Farm Workers Excluding Agricultural Service Workers				
	(in thousands)			(% change)	
	July 2005	July 2006	July 2007	July 2005-July 2006	July 2006-July 2007
United States (excluding AK)	936	876	847	-6.4	-3.3
Hawaii	7	7	6	0.0	-14.3
California	206	191	192	-7.3	0.5
Pacific (OR, WA)	109	92	92	-15.6	0.0
Mountain I (ID, MT, WY)	29	30	22	3.4	-26.7
Mountain II (CO, NV, UT)	26	25	18	-3.8	-28.0
Mountain III (AZ, NM)	24	25	22	4.2	-12.0
Northern Plains (KS, NE, ND, SD)	45	41	40	-8.9	-2.4
Southern Plains (OK, TX)	63	53	58	-15.9	9.4
Delta (AR, LA, MS)	24	30	25	25.0	-16.7
Cornbelt I (IL, IN, OH)	54	55	53	1.9	-3.6
Cornbelt II (IA, MO)	31	23	24	-25.8	4.3
Lake (MI, MN, WI)	75	68	78	-9.3	14.7
Florida	41	43	41	4.9	-4.7
Southeast (AL, GA, SC)	44	41	31	-6.8	-24.4
Appalachian I (NC, VA)	38	40	40	5.3	0.0
Appalachian II (KY, TN, WV)	24	27	30	12.5	11.1
Northeast I (CT, ME, MA, NH, NY, RI, VT)	46	36	39	-21.7	8.3
Northeast II (DE, MD, NJ, PA)	50	49	36	-2.0	-26.5

Source: U.S. Department of Agriculture, National Agricultural Statistics Service, *Farm Labor*, August releases.

Note: See notes in table 1 for definitions of hired farm worker and agricultural service worker.

Hired Farm Workers

When statistics on hired farm workers alone are analyzed, they do not signal a scarcity of farm labor during a period of peak demand. Employment of hired farm workers in the year ended July 2007 fluctuated much like it had previously over time in the 15 regions and 3 states into which NASS divides the United States. (See table 3.) Farmers in eight regions, Florida and Hawaii reduced their demand for direct-hire farm workers this past July. In addition, employment of hired farm workers remained the same between July 2006 and July 2007 in the Pacific region (Oregon, Washington) and Appalachian I region (North Carolina, Virginia). Thus, growers used fewer or the same number of hired farm workers this July in the majority of regions (10 out of 15) and states (2 out of 3) for which the FLS provides data.

Variable climate conditions may explain a good deal of the long-standing yearly fluctuations in farm employment. For example, drought or hurricanes could severely curtail crop production in a given region in one year that would greatly reduce labor requirements; the following year the same area could have more normal weather conditions that would produce a larger crop and, hence, a greater demand for labor. A specific example involves Washington state. Different weather conditions in 2006 than 2005 affected when demand peaked for harvesting cherries, which in turn affected the supply of labor to other growers in the state. As a result of the delayed surge in demand for labor among cherry producers in 2006, many workers who usually would have switched to working for apple growers in August instead continued to harvest cherries. Their analysis led Ernst W. Stromsdorfer and John H. Wines to conclude that

> dramatic year-to-year seasonal changes explain much of the concern of agricultural producers over the adequacy and timeliness of the supply of seasonal agricultural workers.[23]

Unemployment

Employment data paint an incomplete picture of the state of the labor market. At the same time that employment in a given occupation is decreasing or increasing relatively slowly, unemployment in the occupation might be falling. Employers would then be faced with a shrinking supply of untapped labor from which to draw. A falling unemployment rate or level would offer some basis for this possibility.

As shown in table 4, the unemployment rate of hired farm workers engaged in crop or livestock production (including contract labor) is quite high. Even the economic boom that characterized most of the 1990s did not reduce the group's unemployment rate below double-digit levels, or about twice the average unemployment rate in the nation at a minimum. Discouragement over their employment prospects in agriculture or better opportunities elsewhere may have prompted some unemployed farm workers to leave the sector as evidenced by their reduced number after 1998 (see column 4 of the table).

Table 4. The Rate and Level of Unemployment

Year	Unemployment Rate		Number of Unemployed Hired Farm Workers (in thousands)
	All Occupations	Hired Farm Workers	
1994	6.1	12.1	109
1995	5.6	12.5	121
1996	5.4	11.5	118
1997	4.9	10.6	106
1998	4.5	11.8	117
1999	4.2	10.6	100
2000	4.0	10.6	104
2001	4.7	12.1	103
2002	5.8	11.4	102
2003	6.0	12.9	100
2004	5.5	11.4	92
2005	5.1	9.0	72
2006	4.6	9.4	78

Source: CPS data tabulated by the BLS (column 2) and the ERS (columns 3 and 4).
Note: In the CPS, an individual's occupation is based on the activity in which he or she spent the most hours during the survey week. The ERS defines hired farm workers as individuals aged 15 or older whose primary job is farm work and for which they receive wages. Hired farm workers include individuals engaged in crop or livestock production whom growers employ directly or through agricultural service providers (e.g., farm labor contractors), as well as farm managers, supervisors of farm workers, and nursery and other workers.

Other observers have examined the unemployment rates in counties that are heavily dependent on the crop farming industry. The GAO, for example, found that many of these agricultural areas chronically experienced double-digit unemployment rates that were well above those reported for much of the rest of the United States. Even when looking at monthly unemployment rates for these areas in order to take into account the seasonality of farm work, the agency found that the agricultural counties exhibited comparatively high rates of joblessness.[24] These kinds of findings imply a surplus rather than a shortage of farm workers.[25]

Another perspective on the availability of untapped farm labor comes from the DOL's National Agricultural Worker Survey (NAWS). During FY2001 -FY2002, the typical crop worker spent 66% of the year performing farm jobs. The remainder of the year, these farm workers either were engaged in nonfarm work (10% of the year) or not working (16%) while in the United States, or they were out of the country (7%).[26] This pattern also suggests an excess supply of labor, assuming that the workers wanted more farm employment. Grower advocates contend that the pattern is a manifestation of working in a seasonal industry. Even in a month of peak industry demand, however, only a small majority of farm workers hold farm jobs.[27]

Time Worked

Another indicator of supply-demand conditions is the amount of time worked (e.g., hours or days). If employers are faced with a labor shortage, they might be expected to increase the amount of time worked by their employees.

The Seasonality of Demand: Hours Versus Employment

Recent data reveal no discernible year-to-year variation in the average number of weekly hours that hired farm workers are employed in crop or livestock production. According to the FLS, the average workweek of hired farm workers has ranged narrowly around 40.0 hours since the mid-1990s. Thus, neither the trend in employment nor in work hours imply the existence of a farm labor shortage.

There also is not much variability in demand over the course of a year based on hours worked. In 2006, for example, the average week of hired farm workers was 33.2 hours in mid-January, 40.8 hours in mid-April, 41.0 hours in mid-July and 41.6 hours in mid-October. (NASS did not conduct a survey in the first quarter of 2007.)

The instability of the demand for farm labor within a year (i.e., seasonality) is reflected in employment levels more than in work hours per week. The FLS data show that in 2006, for example, farmers had 614,000 workers on their payrolls in mid-January; 720,000 in mid-April; 876,000 in mid-July; and 797,000 in mid-October.

The Number of Days Worked

Another measure of time worked available from the FLS is "expected days of employment" (i.e., farm operators are asked the number of days they intend to utilize their hired farm workers over the course of a year). As shown in table 5, they anticipated a low of 579,000 farm workers on their payrolls for at least 150 days in 2006 and a high of 679,000 (un)authorized workers in 2002. These "year-round" workers typically have accounted for at least three- fourths of hired farm workers in the current decade.[28]

Table 5. Hired Farm Workers by Expected Days of Employment (numbers in thousands)

Year	150 Days or More of Expected Employment		149 Days or Less of Expected Employment
	Number of Hired Workers	Percent of All Hired Farm Workers	
1994	597	71	243
1995	598	69	271
1996	593	71	239
1997	629	72	247
1998	639	73	241
1999	666	72	263
2000	640	72	251
2001	658	75	224
2002	679	77	207
2003	635	76	201
2004	611	74	246
2005	594	76	185
2006	579	77	173

Source: Annual averages calculated by CRS from quarterly releases of the FLS.
Note: See note in table 1 for definition of hired farm worker.

According to the NAWS, the number of actual farm workdays varies by legal status.[29] Unauthorized workers averaged 197 days in crop production, compared to 185 days for authorized workers in FY2001-FY2002. More unauthorized than authorized workers were likely to spend at least 200 days in farm jobs (58% and 50%, respectively). Within the authorized population, citizens averaged 175 days and permanent residents, 195 days of employment in farming during the year.

Wages

As previously stated, economic theory suggests that if the demand for labor is nearing or has outstripped the supply of labor, firms will in the short-run bid up wages to compete for workers. Consequently, earnings in the short-supply field would be expected to increase more rapidly than earnings across all industries or occupations. The ratio of, in this instance, farm to nonfarm wages also would be expected to rise if the farm labor supply were tight.

Table 6. Average Hourly Earnings of Field Workers and Other Workers in the Private Sector (in nominal dollars)

Year	Average Hourly Wages of Field Workers	Average Hourly Wages of Production or Nonsupervisory Workers in the Private Nonfarm Sector	Ratio of Hourly Field Worker Wages to Private Nonfarm Worker Wages
1990	$5.23	$10.20	0.51
1991	5.49	10.52	0.52
1992	5.69	10.77	0.53
1993	5.90	11.05	0.53
1994	6.02	11.34	0.53
1995	6.13	11.65	0.53
1996	6.34	12.04	0.53
1997	6.66	12.51	0.53
1998	6.97	13.01	0.54
1999	7.19	13.49	0.53
2000	7.50	14.02	0.53
2001	7.78	14.54	0.54
2002	8.12	14.97	0.54
2003	8.31	15.37	0.54
2004	8.45	15.69	0.54
2005	8.70	16.13	0.54
2006	9.06	16.76	0.54
1990-2006 change	73.2%	64.3%	—

Source: Created by CRS from FLS (column 2) and BLS (column 3) employer survey data.

Note: Field workers are a subset of hired farm workers who engage in planting, tending and harvesting crops. The data relate to all field workers regardless of method of payment (i.e., those paid an hourly rate, by the piece or a combination of the two). Workers paid directly by agricultural service providers are excluded.

As shown above in table 6, the average hourly earnings of field (excluding contract) workers rose to a greater extent than those of other employees in the private sector between 1990 and 2006, at 73.2% and 64.3%, respectively. Nonetheless, field workers' pay hardly increased compared to other workers' pay: at $9.06 per hour in 2006, field workers still earn little more than 50 cents for every dollar earned by other private sector workers.

An over-the-year comparison of farm and nonfarm wage data for the nation in the peak demand month of July also does not suggest the presence of a labor shortage. As shown in table 7, the hourly wages of field workers increased at an accelerating rate between July 2005-July 2006 and July 2006-July 2007. But, growers generally did not bid up wages to attract workers to a greater degree than employers in other industries.[30]

However, growers in three areas — California, Mountain II (Colorado, Nevada and Utah) and Mountain III (Arizona, New Mexico) — raised wages in July 2007 to a much greater extent than the U.S. average for field workers (4.3%) and for employees in private nonfarm industries (4.1%). It appears that only California's above-average wage increase may have been associated with labor scarcity.

California

The wage rate of field workers in California increased by 9.9% between July 2006 and July 2007. (See table 7.) The wage rate of agricultural service workers employed on the state's farms rose as well (5.4%).[31] These above-average wage increases likely contributed to the state's comparatively high increase of 6.6% in hired farm worker and agricultural service employment in July 2007, as previously shown in table 3. According to the August 2007 *Farm Labor* release of July data, "continued concern [of California growers] about potential labor shortages due to increased border security [led them to pay] ... workers more in order to compete with the higher paying construction industry."

Some southwestern growers also reportedly reacted to the tightening of the farm labor market this summer by

> raising crops across the border where many of the workers are ... Western Growers, an association representing farmers in California and Arizona, conducted an informal survey of its members in the spring. Twelve large agribusinesses that acknowledged having operations in Mexico reported a total of 11,000 workers [t]here.[32]

Table 7. Hourly Wage Rates of Hired Field Workers by Area, July 2005-July 2007

Area	Hourly Wage of Field Workers Excluding Agricultural Service Workers				
	(in current dollars)			(percent change)	
	July 2005	July 2006	July 2007	July 2005-July 2006	July 2006-July 2007
United States (excluding Alaska)	8.61	8.93	9.31	3.7	4.3
Hawaii	10.00	10.26	10.70	2.6	4.3
California	8.76	8.92	9.80	1.8	9.9
Pacific (OR, WA)	8.60	9.50	9.64	10.5	1.5
Mountain I (ID, MT, WY)	8.39	8.41	8.36	0.2	-0.6
Mountain II (CO, NV, UT)	8.62	8.33	9.25	-3.4	11.0
Mountain III (AZ, NM)	7.90	7.55	8.34	-4.4	10.5
Northern Plains (KS, NE, ND, SD)	8.15	8.94	9.13	9.7	2.1
Southern Plains (OK, TX)	8.07	8.53	8.14	5.7	-4.6
Delta (AR, LA, MS)	7.59	8.06	8.14	6.2	0.9
Cornbelt I (IL, IN, OH)	9.20	9.46	9.22	2.8	-2.5
Cornbelt II (IA, MO)	8.86	9.85	9.44	11.2	-4.2
Lake (MI, MN, WI)	8.66	9.37	9.52	8.2	1.6
Florida	8.75	8.39	8.50	-4.1	1.3
Southeast (AL, GA, SC)	8.39	8.21	8.57	-2.1	4.4
Appalachian I (NC, VA)	8.44	9.14	8.80	8.3	-3.7
Appalachian II (KY, TN, WV)	8.46	8.64	8.55	2.1	-1.0
Northeast I (CT, ME, MA, NH, NY, RI, VT)	8.88	9.28	9.58	4.5	3.2
Northeast II (DE, MD, NJ, PA)	8.71	9.26	9.62	6.3	3.9

Source: U.S. Department of Agriculture, National Agricultural Statistics Service, *Farm Labor*, August releases.

Note: A hired field worker is anyone, other than an agricultural service worker, who was paid for at least one hour of work on a farm spent planting, tending and harvesting crops (including operation of farm machinery on crop farms). The figures reflect all ways in which farm workers are paid (e.g., by the hour, by the piece). The wage rate is calculated based on total wages paid and hours worked during the survey week.

This is one of the actions that economists hypothesize employers will take to bring a scarce labor input into balance with demand. It is akin to the offshoring of work engaged in by other U.S. industries. Thus, the farm labor market in California functioned as economists theorize: growers were able to attract more workers by substantially raising wages, and they economized on U.S. labor by offshoring production.

Arizona, Colorado, Nevada, New Mexico and Utah

The well above-average wage increases among field workers shown in table 7 in Mountain II (Colorado, Nevada and Utah) and Mountain III (Arizona, New Mexico) is related to the same factor that pushed up the average hourly wage of all hired farm workers — namely, "a greater percentage of salaried workers putting in fewer hours."[33] The lower demand for labor, evidenced by fewer hours worked, appears due to different climate conditions in July 2007 compared to a year earlier. The reduced employment in Mountain II this past July resulted from the winter wheat harvest "being behind last year's pace," and the lower employment in Mountain III resulted from "abnormally hot and extremely dry weather" that limited activity on farms during the survey's reference week.[34]

CONCLUSION

In summary, indicators of supply-demand conditions generally are inconsistent with the existence of a nationwide shortage of domestically available farm workers in part because the measures include both authorized and unauthorized employment. This finding does not preclude the possibility of farm worker shortages in certain parts of the country at various times during the year. The analysis does not address the adequacy of authorized workers in the seasonal farm labor supply relative to grower demand.

Whether there would be an adequate supply of authorized U.S. farm workers if new technologies were developed or different labor-management practices were implemented continues to be an unanswered question. Whether more U.S. workers would be willing to become farm workers if wages were raised and whether the size of the increase would make the industry uncompetitive in the world marketplace also remain open issues. These matters remain unresolved because perishable crop growers have rarely, if ever, had to operate without unauthorized aliens being present in the domestic farm workforce.[35]

REFERENCES

[1] In this report, the terms "agriculture" and "farming" will be used interchangeably as will the terms "producer," "grower," and "farmer."

[2] Victor J. Oliveira, Anne B. W. Effland, Jack L. Runyan and Shannon Hamm, *Hired Farm Labor on Fruit, Vegetable, and Horticultural Specialty Farms*, U.S. Department of Agriculture, Economic Research Service, Agricultural Economic Report 676, December 1993, p. 2. (Hereafter cited as, Oliveira, Effland, Runyan and Hamm, *Hired Farm Labor on Fruit, Vegetable, and Horticultural Specialty Farms*.)

[3] U.S. Congress, Senate Committee on the Judiciary, *Temporary Worker Programs: Background and Issues*, committee print, 96th Cong., 2nd sess. (Washington: GPO, 1980).

[4] Philip L. Martin, "Good Intentions Gone Awry: IRCA and U.S. Agriculture," *Annals of the American Academy of Political and Social Science*, July 1994.

[5] According to *U.S. Department of Labor Report to Congress: The Agricultural Labor Market — Status and Recommendations*, the 1.8 million figure was developed by dividing the hourly earnings of field and livestock workers into farm labor expenditures to estimate the number of work hours on crop and livestock farms. As it was calculated that 72% of the hours were being worked on crop farms, the percentage was then applied to the Commission on Agricultural Workers' estimate for 1992 of 2.5 million persons employed for wages on U.S. farms to yield a current estimate of the hired crop workforce. The Commission had developed its earlier farm employment figure from a variety of data sources because there is no actual head count of farm workers. For other current estimates of hired farm and crop workers see table 1.

[6] DOL, Findings from the National Agricultural Workers Survey (NAWS) 2001-2002, Research Report No. 9, March 2005. (Hereafter cited as DOL, Findings from the NAWS 2001-2002.)

[7] Commission on Agricultural Workers (CAW), *Report of the Commission on Agricultural Workers*, (Washington: GPO, November 1992). (Hereafter cited as CAW, *Report of the Commission on Agricultural Workers*.). U.S. General Accounting Office (GAO), *H-2A Agricultural Guestworker Program: Changes Could Improve Services to Employers and Better Protect Workers*, GAO/HEHES-98-20, December 1997. (Hereafter cited as GAO, *H-2A Agricultural Guestworker Program*).

DOL, *A Profile of U.S. Farmworkers: Demographics, Household Composition, Income and Use of Services*, Research Report No. 6, April 1997. (Hereafter cited as DOL, *A Profile of U.S. Farmworkers*.) And, annual calculations in the early 1990s by the U.S. Departments of Labor and Agriculture.

[8] The INS approved more than 1 million of the applications that individuals filed under the SAW program to become legal permanent residents. Anticipating that SAWs would leave farming because IRCA did not require them to remain in order to adjust their status, P.L. 99-603 included the RAW program as a back-up measure to ensure growers of an adequate labor supply. The RAW program was never used because the annual calculations of farm labor supply and demand that were made by the U.S. Departments of Labor and Agriculture during the FY1990-FY1993 period found no national shortages of farm workers.

[9] Seasonal agricultural services (SAS) were defined broadly in IRCA as field work related to planting, cultivating, growing and harvesting of fruits and vegetables of every kind and other perishable commodities. The terms "SAS," "seasonal farm work," "field work" and "crop work" are used interchangeably in this report.

[10] CAW, Report of the Commission on Agricultural Workers, p. 75.

[11] DOL, U.S. Farmworkers in the Post-IRCA Period, Research Report No. 4, March 1993. (Hereafter cited as DOL, U.S. Farmworkers in the Post-IRCA Period.)

[12] DOL, Findings from the NAWS 2001-2002.

[13] CAW, Report of the Commission on Agricultural Workers, p. 80.

[14] 2007 email communication from the U.S. Department of Labor.

[15] Alternatively, there are a number of reasons why SAWs would remain in farm employment (e.g., limited English-language fluency and little formal education). In light of these competing factors, the CAW concluded that it would be difficult to estimate the attrition rate of SAWs from the fields. The existence of fraud in the SAW program further complicates such a calculation because the stock of SAWs who genuinely were farm workers is unknown: when Congress was debating immigration proposals in the mid-1980s, the U.S. Department of Agriculture estimated that there were 300,000 to 500,000 unauthorized farm workers, but more than twice the upper-end estimate were legalized under the SAW program; this large discrepancy, as well as additional research, led to the widely held conclusion that fraud was extensive.

[16] The CAW determined that the design of the SAW program was, at least in part, responsible for the increase in unauthorized immigration because if dependents of SAWs did not similarly have their status adjusted, they might have illegally entered the United States to join family members. In addition, the network or kinship recruitment process for SAS work continued to flourish and to facilitate not only job placement, but also migration by assisting in border-crossing and in acquiring fraudulent work authorization documents. These findings led the Commission to conclude that "the concept of a worker-specific and industry-specific legalization program was fundamentally flawed. It invited fraud, posed difficult definitional the longstanding priority of U.S. immigration policy favoring the unification of families." CAW, *Report of the Commission on Agricultural Workers*, p. 67.
[17] DOL, A Profile of U.S. Farmworkers.
[18] DOL, Findings from the National Agricultural Workers Survey: 199 7-1998, Research Report No. 8, March 2000. (Hereafter cited as DOL, Findings from the National Agricultural Workers Survey: 199 7-1998.)
[19] DOL, Findings from the NAWS 2001-2002.
[20] DOL, Farmworkers in the Post-IR CA Period and Findings from the NA WS 2001-2002.
[21] Exceptions are those occupations with very well delineated and widely agreed upon credentials. In the case of registered nurses, for example, the number of students graduating from nursing programs as well as the number of workers in the United States already licensed as registered nurses would compose the available supply of individuals to the occupation.
[22] According to CPS data, nonfarm wage and salary employment averaged 132,449,000 in calendar year 2006 and 133,759,000 in January-July 2007. (Monthly data for 2007 are preliminary and subject to revision.)
[23] Washington State Employment Security Department, "Agricultural Employment and the Issue of a 2006 Seasonal Labor Shortage," *2006 Agricultural Workforce in Washington State*.
[24] GAO, H-2A Agricultural Guestworker Program.
[25] See also testimony of Cecilia Munoz, on behalf of the National Council of La Raza before the Senate Judiciary Subcommittee on Immigration, May 12, 1999.
[26] DOL, Findings from the NAWS 2001-2002.
[27] DOL, Findings from the National Agricultural Workers Survey: 199 7-1998.

[28] These figures potentially are relevant to legislation that would link eligibility for legalization to time spent in farm work. While some might wish to use the above-described data to roughly estimate the number of unauthorized farm workers who would be eligible to adjust status, they describe the *expectations* of farmers and they do not distinguish between legal and illegal workers. In addition, the data could produce an underestimate because they omit the more than 200,000 contract workers on the payrolls of agricultural service providers. Alternatively, the data could produce an overestimate because they include employees not normally thought of as farm workers (e.g., bookkeepers, pilots).

[29] DOL, Findings from the NAWS 2001-2002.

[30] Based on data collected by the U.S. Bureau of Labor Statistics for production and nonsupervisory workers in private nonfarm industries, average hourly earnings grew by 3.9% in 2006 and by 4.1% in the January-July 2007 period. The employees had average hourly earnings of $16.13 in 2005, $16.76 in 2006, and $17.45 in July 2007 (preliminary data subject to revision).

[31] Wage rates of individuals who perform work on farms under a contract or fee arrangement are available from the FLS for only California and Florida. In July 2006, the hourly wage rate of agricultural service workers in California was $9.49; in July 2007, $10.00.

[32] "Short on Labor, Farmers in U.S. Shift to Mexico," *New York Times*, September 5, 2007.

[33] NASS, *Farm Labor*, August 2007, p. 1 and conversation between CRS and NASS staff. NASS calculates wage rates based on total wages paid and hours worked during the survey week. Salaried workers are paid a pre-set sum per week or month, for example, that is not directly linked to their input (unlike hourly workers who are paid based on the number of hours they actually work) or their output (unlike piece-rate workers who are paid based on the amount of crops they harvest).

[34] Conversation between CRS and NASS staff.

[35] In the conference report for the DOL's FY2000 appropriation (H.Rept. 106-479), DOL was charged with reporting on ways to promote a legal farm workforce and on options for such things as improving farm worker compensation and developing a more stable workforce. The report (*U.S. Department of Labor Report to Congress: The Agricultural Labor Market — Status and Recommendations*) was issued in December 2000. Recommendations included continuing appropriations for AgWork (i.e., an internet-based, on-line job matching system specifically for agricultural

employees and employers), encouraging greater use of automated employee verification systems, and further pursuing H-2A program streamlining while maintaining farm worker protections. The report concluded that IRCA's farm legalization program failed to turn an unauthorized into an authorized workforce. It asserted that proposals to ease growers' access to temporary farm workers outside the existing H-2A program "would not create a legal domestic agricultural workforce" and instead "would lower wages and working and living conditions in agricultural jobs resulting in fewer domestic workers continuing employment in agriculture and perpetuating the industry's dependence on a foreign labor force." The report noted that one approach to creating an authorized supply of crop workers had never been tried, namely, increasing wages and improving working conditions "by normalizing legal protections for farm workers and increasing mechanization," which has the potential to attract more U.S. workers to agriculture and raise the productivity of a possibly smaller farm labor force. In recognition that there might be short-run increases in growers' labor costs were these recommendations implemented, DOL urged Congress was urged to consider ways to temporarily assist them.

INDEX

#

9/11, 27, 48

A

abusive, 9
access, 2, 39, 41, 44, 45, 48, 60, 159
accessibility, 122
accidents, 38
accounting, 10, 27
Acquired Immune Deficiency Syndrome, 55
adjustment, 113
administrative, 17, 49, 73, 83
adults, 15
advocacy, 21, 36
African American, 59, 67
African Americans, 67
age, 12, 13, 15, 20, 21, 22, 23, 24, 30, 33, 40, 42, 45, 47, 59, 139, 143
aggregation, 39
aging, 139
agricultural, vii, viii, ix, x, 1, 2, 3, 4, 5, 6, 7, 8, 9, 10, 15, 19, 20, 22, 26, 32, 37, 38, 39, 41, 48, 49, 50, 58, 61, 62, 63, 64, 65, 66, 67, 68, 69, 70, 71, 73, 78, 79, 80, 88, 116, 117, 118, 119, 120, 121, 122, 129, 131, 132, 133, 135, 136, 137, 138, 139, 143, 144, 145, 146, 147, 148, 151, 153, 156, 158

agricultural commodities, 10, 62
agricultural sector, vii, 4, 5, 6, 7, 9, 39, 41, 48, 49, 133, 137
agriculture, 1, 2, 3, 5, 6, 7, 15, 19, 39, 49, 62, 63, 64, 65, 67, 120, 129, 132, 133, 138, 147, 155, 159
aid, 28, 62, 71, 73, 153, 158
AL, 56, 145, 152
Alabama, 57, 75, 81, 96, 123, 127
Alaska, 57, 59, 61, 73, 74, 77, 79, 80, 113, 118, 122, 125, 143, 144, 152
aliens, ix, x, 118, 132, 135, 137, 138, 139, 140, 154
alternative, 122
alternatives, 14
American culture, 119
American Indian, 59
analysts, 27, 139
Animals, 58, 79, 84, 92, 94, 95, 96, 97, 98, 99, 100, 101, 102, 103
application, 37, 112
appropriations, 158
Arizona, 11, 57, 75, 81, 123, 127, 131, 152, 153, 154
Arkansas, 57, 75, 81, 123, 127
ash, 10
Asian, 14, 15, 24, 30, 33, 59, 130
assessment, x, 136
assets, 60, 62
assumptions, 63, 89, 90, 91, 92
Athens, 96

Index

attacks, 137
Attorney General, 121
availability, 9, 43, 121, 122, 139, 147
average earnings, 29

B

bargaining, x, 130, 136, 139
barley, 57
barriers, 4, 23, 41
barriers to entry, 23
benefits, 20, 43, 45, 47, 50, 59, 68, 73, 88, 130
bias, 60
birth, 14, 30, 59
Blacks, 14
bonus, 110
Border Patrol, 67
border security, 49, 153

C

Caribbean, 12, 58
category a, 35, 58
cattle, 58
Census, 4, 6, 7, 11, 39, 52, 56, 57, 59, 60, 61, 63, 64, 114
Census Bureau, 7, 56, 59, 60, 114
Centers for Disease Control, 54
Central America, 12, 58
certification, 20, 71, 72, 112, 114, 121
certifications, 74, 84, 112
channels, 58
cherries, 146
child labor, 15, 67
children, 3, 15, 33, 35, 43, 45, 47, 62
Christmas, 105
Cincinnati, 54, 102
citizens, 3, 12, 17, 22, 45, 58, 115, 119, 131, 150
citizenship, 4, 6, 12, 13, 15, 17, 22, 24, 27, 30, 34, 35, 36, 49, 58, 119
citrus, 57
civilian, 60
classification, 39

collateral, 130
College Station, 131
Colorado, 11, 57, 75, 81, 123, 127, 152, 154
Committee on Appropriations, 133
Committee on the Judiciary, 155
commodity, 10
communication, 156
communities, 14, 15, 50, 114
community, 120, 132
compensation, 9, 20, 22, 28, 35, 43, 44, 46, 50, 72, 126, 129, 130, 158
competition, 120, 122
compliance, 115
composition, 36, 60, 137
concentration, 88
conception, 31
confidence, 60
Congress, viii, ix, 9, 21, 67, 70, 71, 113, 121, 126, 132, 133, 135, 136, 137, 138, 155, 156, 158
Connecticut, 57, 75, 81, 123, 127
Consolidated Appropriations Act, 79
consolidation, 48
construction, 9, 133, 153
Consumer Price Index, 28
consumers, 140
consumption, 7, 48
contractors, 8, 28, 32, 33, 38, 67, 78, 79, 80, 88, 140, 142, 143, 145, 148
contracts, 37
control, 68
Coping, 120
corn, 10, 57, 104
correlation, 50
cost of living, 78
costs, 4, 6, 9, 26, 41, 88, 159
cotton, 57
country of origin, 119
coverage, 23, 43, 45, 50, 61, 82, 126
cows, 113, 143
CPI, 28, 113
CPS, 4, 6, 11, 12, 13, 14, 17, 23, 26, 27, 33, 35, 45, 46, 53, 60, 63, 64, 65, 66, 140, 143, 148, 157
credentials, 157

credit, 35, 37
crop production, 39, 65, 72, 139, 140, 143, 146, 150
crops, x, 3, 5, 9, 10, 23, 57, 58, 64, 80, 113, 136, 139, 143, 144, 151, 153, 158
cross-sectional, 6, 63, 64
CRS, 69, 74, 89, 90, 91, 92, 112, 114, 117, 130, 132, 133, 135, 137, 143, 150, 151, 158
CT, 146, 153
Current Population Survey (CPS), vii, 1, 4, 6, 11, 14, 16, 22, 25, 26, 27, 28, 29, 30, 34, 36, 47, 60, 64, 140
Customs and Border Protection, 21
cycles, 5, 59

D

dairy, 10
data collection, 13, 49, 60
data set, 13, 31, 59, 63
debts, 62
deciduous, 57
definition, 65, 121, 141, 150
dehydration, 41
demand, 5, 9, 21, 48, 59, 67, 78, 88, 120, 136, 137, 138, 141, 144, 146, 147, 148, 149, 150, 151, 153, 154, 156
demographic characteristics, 21, 29, 60
demography, 1
Department of Agriculture, viii, 1, 2, 51, 52, 53, 54, 55, 56, 61, 69, 70, 73, 113, 116, 122, 125, 140, 143, 144, 146, 153, 155, 156
Department of Commerce, 25, 56
Department of Education, 35
Department of Health and Human Services, 5, 54, 56
Department of Homeland Security, 20, 138
deposits, 37
depreciation, 9
developed countries, 119
diets, 50
disability, 43, 46
disabled, 38, 44
disputes, 59, 133

distribution, 3, 10, 11, 12, 13, 24, 29, 30, 58, 79
domestic demand, 50
drinking, 41, 43
drinking water, 41, 43
drought, 146
duration, 25, 130
duties, viii, 70, 78

E

earnings, x, 3, 6, 20, 21, 22, 23, 26, 27, 28, 29, 30, 37, 50, 58, 59, 60, 71, 73, 79, 122, 127, 136, 150, 155, 158
earnings gap, 26, 29
economic boom, 147
economic disadvantage, 12
Economic Research Service, vii, 1, 2, 4, 51, 52, 53, 54, 55, 62, 142, 143, 155
economic theory, 141, 150
economically disadvantaged, vii, 5
education, 35, 51, 55, 133
educational attainment, 15, 21, 35
email, 156
employee compensation, 9
employees, x, 3, 4, 29, 41, 43, 46, 48, 59, 64, 65, 73, 78, 80, 113, 130, 136, 139, 141, 148, 150, 152, 158, 159
employers, viii, ix, x, 9, 20, 58, 61, 67, 68, 69, 70, 71, 72, 73, 74, 78, 79, 80, 83, 84, 86, 87, 88, 105, 109, 111, 114, 116, 117, 118, 119, 120, 122, 126, 130, 132, 135, 136, 138, 140, 141, 143, 148, 152, 153, 159
employment, vii, viii, ix, x, xi, 1, 2, 5, 6, 7, 14, 17, 19, 20, 21, 22, 23, 24, 26, 27, 29, 32, 33, 39, 43, 46, 48, 49, 50, 59, 60, 66, 68, 70, 71, 83, 87, 88, 111, 114, 117, 118, 119, 121, 122, 130, 132, 133, 136, 137, 138, 139, 140, 141, 142, 144, 145, 146, 147, 149, 150, 153, 154, 155, 156, 157, 159
employment status, 5
England, 114
Environmental Protection Agency, 67
equilibrium, 141
ERIC, 51, 55

esters, 113
ETA, 72, 83, 111
ethnicity, 13, 14, 15, 16, 24, 29, 30, 59
Europe, 48, 51
excess supply, 147
Executive Office of the President, 114
exercise, 78
expenditures, 61, 64, 155
exposure, 4, 36, 38, 40, 42, 51, 53
extrapolation, 6, 8

F

Fair Labor Standards Act, 67, 68, 115, 126
family, 3, 6, 7, 8, 26, 37, 45, 60, 63, 65, 80, 143, 157
family members, 3, 6, 7, 8, 37, 45, 63, 65, 80, 157
Farm Bill, 48
Farm Labor Contractor Registration Act, 67, 133
farm size, 7
farmers, x, 3, 6, 7, 8, 21, 39, 65, 67, 73, 78, 80, 88, 116, 136, 139, 143, 144, 149, 153, 158
farming, 33, 79, 80, 84, 139, 147, 150, 155, 156
farms, viii, xi, 7, 8, 15, 28, 41, 58, 61, 64, 65, 66, 67, 69, 70, 71, 73, 88, 116, 136, 137, 143, 144, 145, 153, 154, 155, 158
farmworkers, vii, viii, 1, 2, 3, 4, 5, 6, 7, 8, 9, 10, 11, 12, 13, 14, 15, 17, 18, 19, 21, 22, 23, 24, 25, 26, 27, 28, 29, 30, 31, 32, 33, 34, 35, 36, 37, 38, 40, 41, 42, 43, 44, 45, 46, 47, 48, 49, 50, 57, 58, 59, 60, 61, 62, 63, 64, 65, 66, 67, 70, 71, 78, 83, 84, 87, 88, 116
fast food, 50
fatalities, 39
fatality rates, 39
fear, 5, 37, 63, 138
February, viii, 69, 71, 77, 78, 82, 113, 114, 133
federal government, 126, 133

Federal Insecticide, Fungicide, and Rodenticide Act, 67
Federal Register, 77, 82, 112, 114, 125, 129, 132
fee, 6, 57, 64, 78, 113, 143, 158
feeding, 58
FIFRA, 67
Filipino, 67
financial support, 38, 44
firms, 43, 132, 141, 143, 150
fish, 112
fishing, 33, 39, 65, 79
FLCRA, 67
flow, ix, x, 26, 118, 135
fluctuations, 9, 15, 19, 32, 43, 146
food, 7, 20, 45, 46, 48, 50
food stamp, 45, 46
food stamps, 45, 46
foreign person, 115
foreign producer, 9
foreign-born population, 48
forestry, 33, 39, 58, 65, 79
Forestry, 39, 115
formal education, 156
Fox, 137
Fox Administration, 137
fraud, 156, 157
freezing, 21
fringe benefits, 73, 130
fruits, vii, 1, 2, 5, 9, 48, 50, 57, 140, 156
funding, 38

G

gangs, 50
GAO, 15, 21, 35, 37, 38, 39, 40, 44, 52, 63, 133, 147, 155, 157
gender, 12, 15
gene, 126
General Accounting Office, 155
generalizations, 126
Georgia, 57, 75, 81, 84, 85, 86, 89, 90, 91, 92, 93, 96, 97, 105, 123, 127
Gibbs, 2
globalization, 48

government, x, 35, 38, 39, 43, 79, 126, 133, 136, 138, 140, 141
Government Accountability Office (GAO), 15, 35, 52
GPO, 155
grapes, 10, 57, 133
grazing, 58
Great Depression, ix, 67, 118, 120, 131
Greenhouse, 10, 57, 79, 84, 92, 94, 95, 96, 97, 98, 99, 100, 101, 102, 103
groups, vii, 4, 5, 6, 12, 19, 21, 26, 37, 45, 59, 60, 63, 64, 85, 87, 131, 133, 139, 140
growth, 48, 142, 144, 145
growth rate, 144
guest worker, ix, 117, 118, 119, 120, 132, 133, 135
guest workers, ix, 118, 119, 132, 133
guidelines, 38, 68

H

H_2, 38, 52
H-2A, v, viii, ix, 17, 20, 21, 49, 56, 58, 69, 70, 71, 72, 74, 78, 83, 84, 86, 87, 88, 104, 105, 110, 111, 112, 113, 117, 118, 121, 122, 126, 127, 132, 155, 157, 159
H-2A program, 21, 49, 71, 72, 74, 78, 112, 114, 132, 159
H-2B, 79
harvest, x, 31, 80, 106, 108, 109, 110, 111, 113, 136, 143, 146, 154, 158
harvesting, 38, 57, 63, 78, 104, 105, 110, 136, 143, 146, 151, 153, 156
hatchery, 112
Hawaii, 57, 73, 74, 75, 81, 123, 127, 131, 145, 146, 152
hazards, 5, 38, 40, 41, 45
health, 1, 3, 4, 33, 35, 37, 38, 39, 40, 41, 42, 43, 44, 45, 50
Health and Human Services, 5, 52, 54, 56, 133
health care, 4, 39, 41, 44
health insurance, 33, 35, 43, 45
health problems, 35
health services, 33
hearing, 143
heat, 4, 41
heat exhaustion, 4
heat stroke, 4, 41
hiring, 20
Hispanic, 3, 12, 13, 14, 15, 16, 17, 23, 24, 30, 32, 33, 51, 53, 55, 58
Hispanic population, 3
Hispanics, 15, 29, 60
HIV, 43, 55
HIV/AIDS, 43
hogs, 10, 58
Homeland Security, 20, 138
homeless, 37
Horticulture, 104, 105
House, 36
household, 14, 36, 46, 47, 60, 140
households, 13, 35, 36, 45, 46, 47, 60, 62, 143
housing, vii, 1, 4, 5, 20, 21, 35, 36, 37, 38, 39, 45, 46, 67, 72, 73, 88, 111
hunting, 39
hurricanes, 146

I

Idaho, 57, 75, 81, 123, 127
illegal aliens, 132, 139
Illinois, 57, 75, 81, 123, 127
immigrants, 5, 15, 17, 19, 20, 47, 62, 67, 68, 119, 120, 137
immigration, vii, ix, 1, 3, 9, 17, 26, 48, 49, 50, 88, 117, 118, 119, 120, 135, 136, 137, 156, 157
Immigration and Customs Enforcement, 138
Immigration and Nationality Act (INA), ix, 79, 111, 117, 120
Immigration Reform and Control Act, x, 9, 17, 58, 68, 135, 138
INA, 79, 111
incentive, viii, 70, 83, 88
incidence, 39
income, 62
India, 67
Indiana, 57, 75, 81, 102, 103, 123, 127
indicators, 39, 42, 141, 154

164 Index

indices, 61
individual character, 3
individual characteristics, 3
industrial, 38, 39, 40, 41, 48
industrial restructuring, 48
industrial sectors, 39
industry, x, 2, 20, 21, 38, 39, 50, 58, 60, 65, 66, 120, 135, 136, 138, 139, 147, 153, 154, 157, 159
Infants, 4
inferences, 46
inflation, 85, 114
injuries, 39, 41, 43
injury, 39, 42, 43
innovation, 7, 48
INS, 156
insight, 4
inspection, 4, 35
inspectors, 65, 79
instability, 23, 149
insurance, 20, 43, 44, 45
integration, 114
international migration, 12
internet, 55, 158
interview, 47
interviews, 12, 59, 72
investment, 35, 38
Iraq, 115
IRCA, x, 9, 17, 19, 20, 26, 32, 49, 53, 56, 68, 135, 138, 139, 155, 156, 159

J

January, 24, 64, 73, 112, 113, 135, 143, 149, 157, 158
Japanese, 67, 130
Jefferson, 103
job matching, 158
jobs, x, 19, 20, 23, 32, 49, 58, 59, 67, 72, 115, 122, 132, 136, 139, 141, 147, 150, 159
judgment, 78
Judiciary, 157
jurisdictions, 126

K

Katrina, 115
Kentucky, 57, 75, 81, 84, 85, 86, 89, 90, 91, 92, 93, 102, 103, 111, 123, 128
key indicators, 39

L

labor, vii, ix, x, 1, 2, 3, 4, 5, 6, 7, 8, 9, 10, 11, 12, 14, 15, 17, 19, 21, 22, 23, 25, 26, 27, 29, 32, 33, 35, 38, 39, 41, 48, 49, 50, 57, 59, 60, 61, 62, 63, 64, 66, 67, 70, 71, 73, 79, 80, 84, 87, 88, 112, 113, 114, 117, 118, 119, 120, 121, 122, 131, 132, 133, 135, 136, 137, 138, 139, 140, 141, 142, 143, 144, 145, 146, 147, 148, 149, 150, 151, 152, 153, 154, 155, 156, 159
labor force, vii, 1, 2, 3, 5, 7, 10, 12, 15, 22, 25, 29, 39, 60, 66, 137, 138, 139, 140, 159
labor markets, 87, 88, 121, 141
labor productivity, 7
labor-intensive, vii, 1, 2, 5, 9, 10, 48
Lafayette, 98
language, 4, 21, 41, 44, 48, 130, 156
language barrier, 4, 41
Latin America, 14, 67
Latino, 13, 51, 58
law, 49, 67, 87, 88, 115, 120
laws, 28, 37, 61
lawsuits, 130
layoffs, 23
lead, 107
learning, 35
legal permanent residents, 20, 156
legal protection, 15, 49, 159
legislation, 20, 21, 48, 49, 113, 133, 138, 158
legislative, 15, 49, 138
lettuce, 133
likelihood, 17, 32, 37, 50
limitation, 6
linear, 6, 8
literacy, 60

Index

livestock, viii, 3, 6, 10, 13, 23, 25, 26, 27, 28, 31, 33, 39, 45, 58, 59, 61, 63, 64, 67, 70, 72, 73, 78, 80, 83, 85, 86, 87, 89, 113, 116, 122, 142, 143, 147, 148, 155
living arrangements, 13
living conditions, 48, 159
local community, 132
local labor markets, 78, 88
location, 31, 32
logging, 65
long-term, 40
Los Angeles, 131
Louisiana, 57, 75, 81, 84, 85, 86, 89, 90, 91, 92, 93, 98, 99, 123, 128
low-level, 120

M

machinery, 38, 113, 153
Madison, 131
Maine, 57, 75, 81, 123, 128
maintenance, 105, 106
management, viii, x, 9, 59, 70, 78, 79, 133, 136, 139, 154
management practices, x, 9, 136, 139, 154
manufacturing, 9
market, vii, x, 1, 2, 3, 5, 6, 19, 32, 48, 49, 110, 111, 130, 136, 140, 142, 144, 147, 153
markets, x, 136, 140
Maryland, 57, 75, 81, 124, 128
Massachusetts, 57, 75, 81, 124, 128
meals, 20, 45, 72, 73
measurement, 65
measures, 141, 154
median, 15, 22, 26, 58
Medicaid, 4, 39, 45, 46, 47, 62
medical care, 38
Medicare, 45, 46
melons, 57
membership, 22
men, 12, 33, 35
mental health, 50
mental illness, 43
Mexican, ix, 9, 13, 54, 55, 67, 118, 119, 120, 131

Mexican Americans, 131
Mexico, ix, 11, 12, 14, 30, 55, 57, 58, 67, 76, 82, 118, 119, 120, 122, 124, 128, 131, 132, 135, 152, 153, 154, 158
Miami, 100
migrant, 1, 3, 5, 15, 31, 32, 33, 35, 38, 39, 50, 60, 61, 67
migrant workers, 31, 35, 50
migrants, 12, 23, 31, 35, 63
migration, 12, 26, 31, 32, 67, 157
military, 120
milk, 57, 113, 143
mines, 119
minimum wage, viii, ix, 9, 20, 21, 28, 61, 67, 69, 70, 71, 72, 74, 80, 82, 83, 84, 86, 87, 105, 109, 111, 113, 115, 117, 118, 122, 126, 127, 133
Minnesota, 57, 76, 81, 124, 128
Mississippi, 57, 76, 81, 124, 128
Missouri, 57, 76, 81, 124, 128
misunderstanding, 130
mobility, 17, 19, 21, 32
money, 15
Monroe, 98
Montana, 57, 76, 81, 124, 128
Montenegro, 51
motion, 119
movement, 9, 119, 121
MSPA, 37
musculoskeletal, 40, 42

N

nation, 137, 142, 144, 147, 151
national, 5, 13, 26, 35, 36, 40, 59, 61, 63, 66, 67, 145, 156
National Institute for Occupational Safety and Health, 38, 54
nationality, 59
Native American, 14, 15, 24, 30, 66
Native Americans, 66
Native Hawaiian, 59
Nebraska, 57, 76, 81, 124, 128
network, 157
Nevada, 57, 76, 82, 124, 128, 152, 154

New England, 73, 114
New Jersey, 57, 76, 82, 124, 128
New Mexico, 11, 55, 57, 76, 82, 124, 128, 131, 152, 154
New Orleans, 98
New York, 51, 53, 54, 55, 57, 73, 76, 82, 124, 128, 131, 158
New York Times, 158
nonimmigrants, 20
Norfolk, 95
normal, 120, 146
North America, 114
North Carolina, 3, 50, 51, 52, 55, 57, 76, 82, 84, 85, 86, 89, 90, 91, 92, 93, 94, 95, 104, 124, 128, 146
Northeast, 11, 26, 27, 57, 146, 153
nurses, 157
nursing, 157
nutrition, 50
nuts, 9, 57

O

occupational, 4, 5, 21, 34, 38, 39, 40
occupational health, 39
occupational mobility, 21
Occupational Safety and Health Act, 67
Office of Management and Budget, 114, 115
Ohio, 57, 76, 82, 102, 124, 128
Oklahoma, 57, 76, 82, 124, 128
olives, 57
OMB, 114
on-line, 158
operator, 38, 61, 62, 65, 106, 110
Operators, 50, 89, 90, 91, 92, 94, 95, 96, 97, 98, 99, 100, 101, 102, 103
opportunity costs, 26
Oregon, 3, 50, 57, 73, 76, 82, 124, 128, 146
organic, 48
organization, 36, 61
orientation, 31
overtime, 22, 23, 28, 58, 67

P

Pacific, 59, 145, 146, 152
Pacific Islander, 59
Pacific Islanders, 59
Pakistan, 67
Panama, 101, 130
paper, 50, 53
parents, 15, 59
payroll, 26
peak demand, 144, 146, 151
peanuts, 58
penalties, x, 9, 136, 139
pendulum, 119
Penn State University, 52
Pennsylvania, 31, 51, 57, 76, 82, 124, 128
percentile, 72, 112
perception, 138
perceptions, 19
periodic, 59
permanent resident, 126, 131, 150
permit, vii, 1, 2, 3, 4, 5, 45
personal, 59
pesticide, 37, 38, 40, 42, 67
pesticides, 4, 5, 35, 36, 40, 41, 42
Philadelphia, 31, 52
pilots, 143, 158
plants, 58, 105, 110
play, 2, 126
policymakers, 48, 78
political refugees, 58
poor, 4, 14
population, vii, 1, 3, 4, 5, 7, 12, 14, 16, 26, 35, 40, 41, 43, 45, 48, 50, 59, 60, 62, 63, 119, 150
port of entry, 21
potato, 104
potatoes, 58
poultry, 58, 113, 143
poverty, vii, 1, 4, 33, 35, 46
poverty rate, 4, 33, 35, 46
power, 139
president, 133
President Bush, 49, 137
prices, 140

Index

private, x, 61, 136, 150, 152, 158
private sector, x, 136, 150
probability, 60
producers, 9, 67, 136, 138, 139, 146, 147
production, vii, 1, 2, 5, 7, 9, 10, 22, 32, 38, 39, 49, 58, 59, 62, 63, 65, 72, 80, 84, 118, 119, 129, 142, 143, 147, 148, 154, 158
productivity, 2, 48, 85, 159
profit, 58
profitability, 9
program, viii, x, 9, 20, 21, 38, 39, 44, 49, 58, 67, 68, 69, 70, 71, 72, 74, 78, 79, 112, 114, 120, 131, 132, 135, 137, 138, 139, 156, 157, 159
promote, 158
proxy, 141
pruning, 57
public, 9, 38, 45, 46, 48, 49, 59, 61, 68, 119, 133
public housing, 46
public policy, 119, 133
public service, 45, 46

Q

qualifications, 121
query, 140
questionnaires, 60, 61

R

race, 13, 29, 58, 59
racial categories, 59
radius, 31
random, 39, 65
range, 9, 29, 48, 62, 67, 80, 110, 126, 143
RAW, 138, 156
real wage, 26
recession, 142
recognition, 159
reduction, 127
reflection, 43
reforms, 49
regional, 74, 78, 122

registered nurses, 157
regular, 45, 61, 126
regulation, 15, 111
regulations, viii, 4, 37, 39, 49, 50, 61, 69, 71, 78, 80, 87, 121, 132
relationship, 141
reliability, 34, 36, 47
rent, 37
repair, 38
repatriation, ix, 118, 131
research, 4, 9, 36, 39, 45, 50, 59, 156
researchers, 59, 63
residential, 17, 36
responsibilities, 130
retail, 140
Rhode Island, 57, 76, 82, 125, 129
rice, 57
risk, x, 4, 39, 67, 136, 138, 139
risks, 5, 38
Rome, 97
rural, 3, 5, 14, 15, 35, 37
rural areas, 3, 5
rural communities, 15
rye, 57

S

safeguards, 15
safety, 37, 39
salaries, 22, 61
salary, 3, 4, 6, 12, 13, 14, 15, 17, 22, 23, 24, 25, 26, 27, 29, 30, 31, 37, 43, 45, 48, 58, 59, 66, 73, 142, 144, 157
sales, 7
Salinas Valley, 51
sample, 60, 65, 72, 79, 84, 105, 109, 111, 116, 140
sample survey, 65
sampling, 116
sampling error, 116
sanctions, x, 135, 138
sanitation, 4, 35
SAS, x, 135, 136, 138, 139, 156, 157
scarcity, 146, 152
school, 3, 4, 14, 15, 22, 24, 30, 35, 45, 120

school meals, 45
schooling, 23
searching, 23
seasonality, 23, 147, 149
Seattle, 130
security, 49, 50, 130, 153
self-employed, 3, 6, 8, 63, 65, 143
Senate, 133, 155, 157
September 11, 137
series, 6, 20, 126, 140
service provider, 116, 143, 148, 151, 158
services, vii, x, 1, 4, 33, 44, 45, 46, 48, 57, 58, 60, 61, 68, 73, 113, 121, 135, 138, 143, 156
sex, 34
sexually transmitted disease, 50
sexually transmitted diseases, 50
shareholders, 61
sharing, 37
sheep, 57, 58, 113, 143
shelter, 37
short supply, 37
shortage, x, 132, 136, 137, 138, 139, 140, 141, 142, 147, 148, 149, 151, 154
SIC, 39
signals, 141
signs, 142
skills, 115, 119
skin, 40, 42
social integration, 114
Social Security, 39, 44, 138
social services, vii, 1, 4, 45, 46, 48, 60, 68
social welfare, 46
socioeconomic, 4, 6
soil, 78
South America, 12, 58
South Carolina, 57, 76, 82, 125, 129
South Dakota, 57, 76, 82, 125, 129
soybeans, 10, 57
speculation, 137
sporadic, ix, 118
stability, 138
standards, 20, 37, 50, 67, 72, 113, 115, 119
statistics, 6, 23, 37, 39, 62, 140, 143, 144, 146
statutory, 126
stock, 156

streams, 5
strikes, 133
stroke, 4, 41
structural changes, 7
students, 35, 157
subgroups, 63
substance abuse, 50
sugar, 58
summer, 15, 64, 137, 153
supervisor, 61, 107, 110
supervisors, 23, 25, 27, 58, 65, 73, 79, 143, 148
supplemental, 26
supply, x, 9, 20, 26, 37, 59, 68, 78, 88, 119, 135, 136, 137, 138, 139, 141, 144, 146, 147, 148, 150, 154, 156, 157, 159
Surgeon General, 54
surplus, ix, 118, 141, 147
switching, 49
systems, 39, 118, 126, 133, 159

T

target population, 35, 62
taxes, 26, 73, 78
technical assistance, 2
technological change, 48
temporary worker visas, 72
Tennessee, 57, 76, 82, 96, 102, 125, 129
tenure, 36
terrorist, 137
terrorist attack, 137
testimony, 133, 157
Texas, 3, 10, 11, 50, 55, 56, 57, 76, 82, 125, 129, 131
threat, ix, 41, 117, 118
time, viii, ix, x, 3, 5, 7, 21, 22, 23, 25, 26, 27, 30, 32, 39, 40, 41, 42, 49, 58, 59, 60, 63, 69, 70, 71, 73, 78, 85, 117, 118, 120, 121, 122, 126, 136, 137, 138, 139, 140, 141, 142, 146, 147, 148, 149, 158
tobacco, 57, 86, 104
tomato, 106
total employment, 24
tourism, 126

Index 169

tourist, 58, 126
tradition, 119
training, 42, 120
trans, 22
transformation, 12
transition, 50
transportation, 20, 67, 72, 88
travel, 31, 32
trees, 58
trend, 9, 14, 19, 39, 141, 142, 149
tuberculosis, 43
turnover, 6, 138
typology, 39

U

U.S. Citizenship and Immigration Services (USCIS), 20, 112
U.S. Department of Agriculture (USDA), viii, 2, 51, 52, 53, 54, 55, 56, 61, 69, 70, 73, 113, 116, 125, 140, 143, 144, 146, 153, 155, 156
U.S. economy, 48, 49, 119
unauthorized workers, vii, x, 1, 4, 5, 6, 9, 17, 26, 27, 29, 36, 37, 41, 46, 49, 61, 63, 68, 88, 135, 136, 138, 139, 140
unemployment, x, 3, 23, 25, 45, 60, 136, 137, 140, 141, 147
unemployment rate, x, 3, 23, 136, 147
unification, 157
unions, 21, 23
United States, vii, viii, ix, x, 1, 2, 3, 4, 5, 9, 10, 12, 13, 14, 17, 18, 20, 21, 30, 31, 32, 38, 48, 49, 50, 51, 52, 53, 54, 55, 56, 58, 59, 61, 63, 67, 68, 69, 70, 71, 79, 83, 88, 111, 112, 113, 115, 116, 117, 118, 119, 120, 121, 122, 130, 131, 132, 135, 137, 138, 141, 144, 145, 146, 147, 152, 157
USCIS, 112
USDA, 6, 8, 20, 28, 35, 37, 38, 53, 54, 56, 66, 70, 71, 73
Utah, 57, 76, 82, 125, 129, 152, 154

V

vacation, 59
Valencia, 110
variability, 149
variable, 140
variables, 133
variation, 50, 64, 144, 148
vegetables, vii, 1, 2, 5, 9, 31, 48, 50, 57, 140, 156
Vermont, 57, 76, 82, 125, 129
veterinarians, 113
visa, 17, 20, 21, 38, 49, 58, 72
visas, 21, 58, 72, 88, 112
vulnerability, 35

W

wage level, viii, 70, 79, 83, 84, 87, 90, 92, 93, 115
wage rate, viii, ix, 20, 61, 64, 69, 70, 71, 72, 73, 74, 79, 80, 83, 84, 85, 89, 90, 91, 92, 93, 115, 117, 118, 119, 121, 122, 129, 130, 133, 153, 158
wages, viii, ix, x, 17, 20, 23, 24, 26, 28, 33, 45, 49, 58, 59, 62, 68, 70, 71, 73, 74, 78, 79, 83, 84, 85, 86, 87, 88, 114, 117, 118, 119, 121, 122, 126, 127, 132, 136, 137, 139, 140, 141, 143, 148, 150, 151, 152, 153, 154, 155, 158, 159
war, 9, 120, 131
war years, 131
water, 41, 43
web, 60
well-being, 6, 17, 62
wheat, 57, 154
wheezing, 42
winter, 64, 131, 154
Wisconsin, 57, 77, 82, 125, 129, 131
women, 33, 35
workforce, viii, ix, x, 2, 9, 12, 14, 29, 31, 39, 50, 60, 70, 71, 78, 117, 118, 135, 136, 137, 138, 154, 155, 158

working conditions, ix, 12, 17, 20, 48, 67, 71, 114, 117, 118, 121, 122, 139, 159
working groups, vii, 5
workplace, 38, 130
World War, ix, 7, 9, 67, 118, 119, 131, 137
Wyoming, 57, 77, 82, 125, 129

Y

yield, 6, 64, 66, 116, 155